I0752714

IMAGES
of America

MIDDLETOWN VALLEY

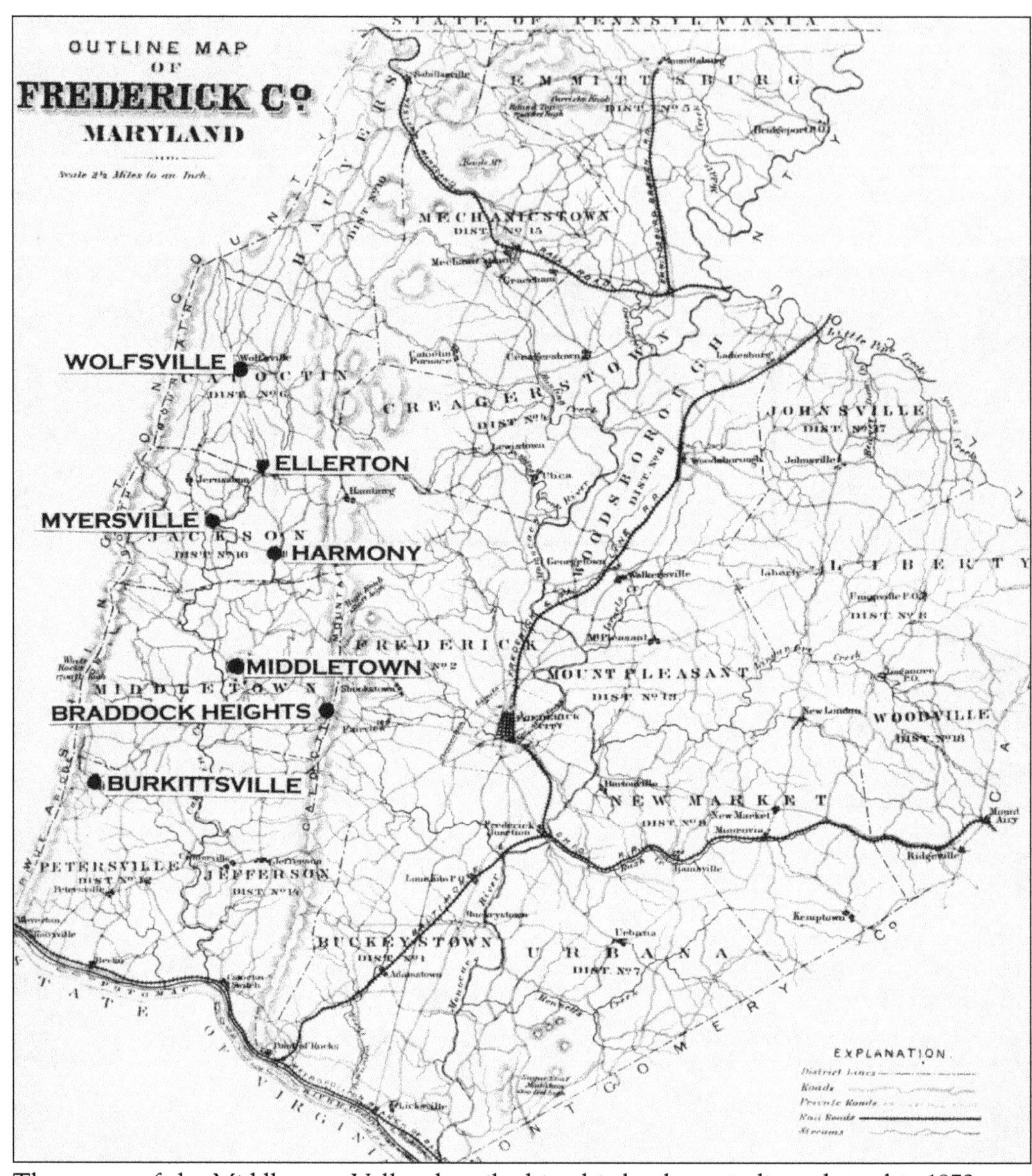

The towns of the Middletown Valley described in this book are indicated on this 1873 map from C.O. Titus and Company's *Atlas of Frederick County, Maryland.* (Courtesy of C.O. Titus and Company.)

On the Cover: In 1926, a total of 800 descendants of early Myersville settler George S. Harp gathered for the Harp Family Pilgrimage. The day's activities included music, prayer, lectures, and family gatherings. (Courtesy of the Summers family.)

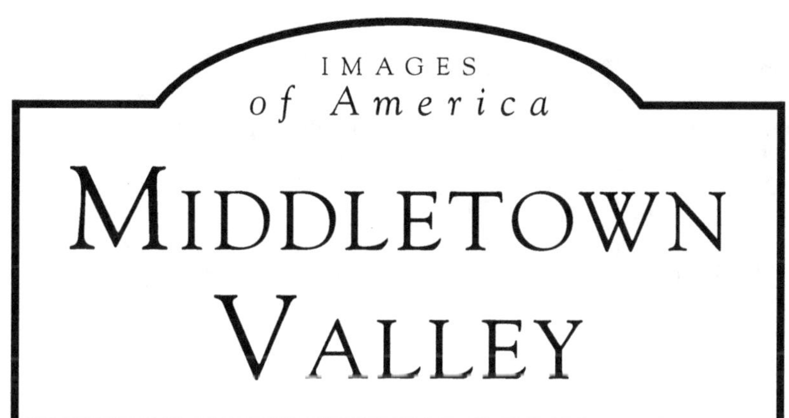

Robert P. Savitt

ISBN 978-1-5316-6575-3

Published by Arcadia Publishing
Charleston, South Carolina

Library of Congress Control Number: 2012936003

For all general information, please contact Arcadia Publishing:
Telephone 843-853-2070
Fax 843-853-0044
E-mail sales@arcadiapublishing.com
For customer service and orders:
Toll-Free 1-888-313-2665

Visit us on the Internet at www.arcadiapublishing.com

For Rindi, Jordan, Brian, Amy, Quinn, Melo, and Janesley:
may you find contentment and fulfillment in your own magic valleys.

Contents

ACKNOWLEDGMENTS

There should be another name on the authorship line of this book. My wife, Babs, refuses to take credit, but this book could not have been prepared without her hard work, talent, and charm in making contacts, meeting with people, and gathering information and images. She will know what I mean when I say that she is "The Woman."

Preparing this book enabled us to meet many wonderful folks in this valley we now call home. We were welcomed into homes, attics, historical societies, and libraries in each of the towns. Many people shared their knowledge, experiences, albums, and scrapbooks, including Jody Brumage, Bill McCutcheon Sr., Kathy Falkenstein, Frances Draper, Virginia Draper, Sue Slimmer, Kurt Bittle, Carroll Leatherman, Debbie and Robert Wilson, George Harne, Elvin Leatherman, Joann Horine, a person who insists on remaining anonymous, Greg Holson, Mary Specht, Anna Mae Wisner, Adrienne Rhoderick, John C. Gladhill, Kathleen Rudisill, Doug Bast, Ann Brown, Mary Mannix, Kathy Gaver, Nancy Chu, Annabelle Martin, Sherry Kemp, Tracy Wiser, David Howell, Tim Ritchey Martin, Stanley Kline, Debbie Bussard, Ester Summers, Dick Phelps, Anna Mae Doub, Judy Zeck, Ray Hinkle, Arthur Leatherman, Harold Stotelmyer, Patricia Wolfe, Don Easterday, Dorothy Buhrman, Wayne and Karen Grossnickle, Patty Ricketts, Eleanor Bittle, Thelma Neel, Debbie Burgoyne, David Somerlade, Paul Gilligan, Patty and Jeff Hurwitz, Kathy Gaver, Janet Main Young, Richard and Pat Pry, Nancy Geasey, Patty and Brent Blickenstaff, Wayne and Pat Guyton, Pat Ropp, Dixie Morgan, Violet Brandenburg, Evelyn Haines, George Brigham, Joyce Coblenz, Elizabeth and Walter Barkdoll, Joyce Brown, Shelby Beaver, Richard DeLauter, and Dale DeLauter.

Among the institutions that provided invaluable assistance were the Middletown Valley Historical Society, the South Mountain Heritage Society, the Maryland Historical Trust, the Braddock Heights Historical Society, the Maryland Room of the Frederick County Public Library, the Western Maryland Room of the Washington County Free Library, Brethren Historical Library and Archives, the Historical Society of Frederick County, and the Central Maryland Heritage League.

A number of works were of particular value in doing research for this book, including George C. Rhoderick Jr.'s *The Early History of Middletown, Maryland*; T.J.C. Williams and Folger McKinsey's *History of Frederick County, Maryland*; Ira C. Moser, Thomas Rose, and Charles S. Martin's *The History of Myersville*; Charles S. Martin and Tom Rose's *The History of Wolfsville and the Catoctin District*; Anne B. Hooper's *Braddock Heights*; and the many books by Virginia Draper on the northern Middletown Valley.

I am sure that I have omitted many names from this acknowledgment section, but my deep gratitude extends to all the kind and gracious people without whom this book would not have been possible.

Introduction

Decades before the American Revolution, pioneers traveling along ancient Indian trails from Pennsylvania into Maryland crested a mountain and came upon a scene that must have reminded them of their Germanic homeland. Before them, in the words of Ira C. Moser, a chronicler of the area's history, "was an unbroken wilderness, clothed with verdure sweeping over hill and dale in billowy undulations, indented here and there by innumerable ravines or cut into narrow leafy rifts by sparkling streams that glowed and glittered in the sunlight."

These brave souls carved out farms and settlements from this wilderness and were joined by others moving south through the fertile valley. Soon after our nation was formed, the National Road emerged, stretching westward from Baltimore across Catoctin Mountain through the valley, the village of Middletown, and over South Mountain. Andrew Jackson, a frequent traveler on this road, described the Middletown Valley of Maryland as "one of the most favored and delightful spots on earth."

Nearly 200 years later, the road traveled by our seventh president still winds through these verdant Maryland hills and continues to enthrall residents and visitors with its magnificent views and culturally rich towns.

The communities of the Middletown Valley bear the imprint of important events in early American history: the French and Indian War, the Revolutionary War, the Civil War, and the building of the National Road as America expanded westward. As these events unfolded around them, local residents went about their lives, building towns and villages with churches and stores, farming the fertile soil, raising livestock, and engaging in rural enterprises such as milling, shoemaking, blacksmithing, furniture making, and distilling.

As the United States entered the 20th century, the Middletown Valley retained its rural character and charm while adapting to a mechanized world. Agriculture remained prominent as farmers began to incorporate modern machinery and techniques. An electric railway line connected the valley's towns with two nearby hub cities, greatly facilitating travel and providing the valley's farmers with a fast and efficient route to bring their produce to markets. This modern transportation line also lured tourists, who began to discover the charms of the refreshingly cool heights of Catoctin Mountain.

The valley's largest settlement, Middletown, has been a center of historic and cultural activity since its founding in the mid-1700s. In 1862, as Confederate forces under Gen. Stonewall Jackson marched along Main Street, 17-year-old Nancy Crouse refused to relinquish her Union flag until forced at gunpoint. Two years later, Confederate forces under Gen. Jubal Early occupied Middletown and forced the payment of a ransom in retaliation for Union actions in southern towns.

Middletown caught the fancy of several US presidents in addition to Andrew Jackson. Col. Rutherford B. Hayes, who would later become the 19th president, gratefully recalled weeks spent in Middletown recuperating from wounds suffered during the nearby Battle of South Mountain. William B. McKinley, the future 25th president, served in the Middletown Valley during that Civil War battle. Years later, Main's Ice Cream store, with its signature grape nut and orange-pineapple flavors, pleased the pallets of chief executives on their way to and from the Camp David presidential retreat.

Myersville, located several miles north of Middletown, was settled in the 1740s by industrious immigrants who set up a bustling community of farmers, craftsmen, and merchants. The little village saw a surge of economic growth in the late 1890s and early 1900s with the extension of the electric railway line from Middletown to Myersville and on to Hagerstown.

The picturesque nearby village of Harmony gained some notoriety during the Revolutionary War when British loyalists were discovered to be plotting to pass along strategic information to the Redcoat army. American forces from nearby Frederick reached the area in time to catch the plotters. Ellerton, a few miles down the road, once boasted several stores and businesses, along with a beautiful waterfall area used by locals for picnics and gatherings.

Braddock Spring, east of Middletown, was a stopping point for British general Edward Braddock's army in 1855 as it traveled along an ancient Indian path on the way to a disastrous defeat at Fort Duquesne during the French and Indian War. Braddock's aide, Col. George Washington, had laid out the route two years earlier. The construction of the electric railway line from Frederick 150 years later led to the creation of the town of Braddock Heights in the cool hills above the spring. The Heights became a resort getaway, with a grand hotel, large boardinghouses and cottages, and attractions like a skating rink, bowling alleys, amusement rides, and an observatory with views of four states.

Neither the trolley nor the main road reached tiny Wolfsville, but its "downtown" area once housed several small businesses and it served as a rural center for the northern Middletown Valley. The village was an early religious center and saw some action during the Civil War when it was occupied by soldiers from General Early's army in 1864.

Burkittsville, in the southern part of the valley, was a bustling town in the 1800s, serving the area's mostly agricultural community. One of the country's best-known distilleries operated near the village, and the town's largest building was home to a female seminary in the mid-1800s. Journalist and writer George Alfred "Gath" Townsend settled in the hills above Burkittsville and erected the world's only monument to war correspondents.

Ghosts and other paranormal beings are no strangers to the Middletown Valley. Perhaps the most enduring and—to local residents—endearing critter mythically inhabiting the valley is the Snallygaster. While the strange beast was the stuff of legend for many years, it came to prominence in the valley in 1909 when George C. Rhoderick, owner of the area's popular weekly newspaper, the *Valley Register*, decided to have some fun with the local legend. He and Ralph S. Wolfe ran a series of stories describing local sightings of the winged beast. T.C. Harbaugh, a former valley resident and widely known writer, described the creature as having two huge wings, a large horny head, and a 20-foot tail. Local residents embellished the tale to fit their own fancies and uses—like encouraging good behavior from their children—and the "monster" became a virtual Middletown Valley mascot that endures to this day.

For three centuries, the daily lives of Middletown Valley residents have been marked by deep traditions owing to their cultural backgrounds, religious activities, occupations, festivals, and sporting endeavors. This book explores the unique history of the people who have lived and worked in this magical valley.

One
Braddock Heights

"This is the place, I cried." With these words, uttered in August 1896 on a plateau overlooking two beautiful valleys, the resort town of Braddock Heights was born.

So it goes, according to Folger McKinsey, the *Baltimore Sun*'s beloved "Bard of Bentztown." McKinsey, the fabled columnist, poet, and friend of Walt Whitman, was invited by George W. Smith, the founder of the Frederick and Middletown Railway Company, to accompany him on a carriage ride to the top of Catoctin Mountain, which overlooks Frederick and Middletown. Smith was seeking a spot to realize a 20-year dream, and he invited McKinsey to help him choose it.

The location afforded magnificent views of the Middletown and Monocacy Valleys; a cool, breezy climate; and accessibility via the National Road and by trolley service from Frederick and, later, Hagerstown. Smith's vision was a colony of summer cottages, hostelries, and accompanying amenities to lure vacationers and day-trippers from nearby cities and towns. Over the years, attractions included a dance pavilion, a theater, a roller-skating rink, bowling alleys, a miniature passenger train, a swimming pool, a café, a park and playground, and an observatory with a view of four states.

Homes and cottages were soon built, and in 1905, a full-service resort hotel opened near the trolley station. The 70-room Hotel Braddock boasted a huge three-sided porch, an open fireplace in the lobby, manicured gardens with walkways, lounges with scenic picture windows, a top-flight restaurant, and telephone and telegraph service. The Hotel Braddock hosted elite guests from Washington, Baltimore, and farther until a devastating fire destroyed it in 1929.

Braddock Heights continued as a summer resort during the Depression and World War II. In the postwar years, traffic on the National Road was significantly reduced when a modern alternative was built several miles north. The trolley closed, and Braddock Heights declined as an amusement area. But local citizens were not about to abandon their scenic mountaintop community. Through careful restoration efforts, Braddock Heights has been industriously reinvented as a charming and vibrant residential community.

In May 1755, British general Edward Braddock led an unsuccessful—and, for him, fatal—expedition to capture Fort Duquesne during the French and Indian War.He was joined in Frederick by the man who would become our nation's first president, George Washington, who served as his aide-de-camp. As the troops climbed Catoctin Mountain, they stopped for refreshment at a spring that was later memorialized as Braddock Spring. (Above, courtesy of Bill McCutcheon; below, courtesy of the Rhoderick family.)

The crest of Catoctin Mountain was chosen as the site for the Braddock Heights resort because of its cool summer weather and stunning views of the Middletown and Monocacy (Frederick) Valleys. In the above image, likely taken in the early 1900s, the Braddock Heights community is in the foreground. In the distance are the fertile hills of the Middletown Valley and the church spires of the town of Middletown. The view below looks down Catoctin Mountain towards the city of Frederick in the distance. (Both, courtesy of Bill McCutcheon.)

The first attraction constructed at Braddock Heights Park, in 1894, was the observatory. This four-floor structure stood 40 feet high and offered a spectacular view. On a clear day, visitors could see four states: Maryland, Virginia, Pennsylvania, and West Virginia. The observatory became the signature site of the new park. Photographs of and from the tower appeared on postcards and in publications, illustrating the pastoral beauty of the resort and its surroundings. The observatory was rebuilt in 1931 and remained a familiar area calling card until it was finally torn down in the 1970s. (Left, courtesy of the Rhoderick family; below, courtesy of Bill McCutcheon.)

No. 19. The Sliding Board and the Observatory, Braddock Heights, Md.

One of the earliest and enduringly popular attractions constructed at Braddock Heights was the wooden sliding board (above). The undulating ripples added a bit of bounce to the ride down, making it irresistible to children—and adults. The slide stood beneath the observatory. In 1926, the wooden surface was replaced by tin and a roof was added to shield sliders from the heat of the sun, as seen below. A sawdust pit was constructed at the bottom of the slide to soften the impact at the end of the run. Riders sometimes slid on wax paper to increase their speed of descent. (Both, courtesy of Bill McCutcheon.)

The initial trolley station stood at Braddock Junction, near the end of the ascent from the Frederick Valley, below Maryland Avenue and the future site of the Hotel Braddock. The first passenger trip, in August 1896, stimulated enormous interest and led to a terrifying accident—in the second weekend of operation, an overloaded trolley car careened down the mountain after its brakes failed. (Courtesy of Bill McCutcheon.)

The first plats in the new resort community were laid out in 1900, and residential construction soon commenced. The first homes—termed "cottages" despite their large size—were built near the trolley stop at Braddock Junction. This photograph, taken in the early years of Braddock Heights, shows some of the cottages along the newly macadamized Maryland Avenue. (Courtesy of Braddock Heights Historical Society.)

The gem of the resort was the luxurious Hotel Braddock, erected in 1905 by Patrick Long, the manager of the popular City Hotel in Frederick. The new hostelry, originally three stories high, stood across from the trolley station and was situated to provide breathtaking views of the Middletown and Monocacy Valleys. Note the enthusiastic message penned by the writer of the postcard. (Author's collection.)

The hotel boasted 70 well-appointed outside rooms and suites with modern plumbing, electric lights, sumptuous meals, and commodious public spaces for lounging, talking, writing, or simply relaxing. As seen here, an additional sleeping floor was added in 1925. The hotel was destroyed by a fire in 1929 and, with the onset of the Great Depression, was not rebuilt. (Courtesy of Bill McCutcheon.)

Since the Braddock Heights area had been largely farmland before the construction of the trolley line and resort community, there were relatively few trees to obstruct the views and cool breezes. The porch of the Hotel Braddock was laid out on three sides, each affording majestic panoramas of the valleys and mountains. The front porch (above) looked past the trolley station towards the Frederick area. Inside the hotel, much of the public area was positioned to take advantage of the bucolic views. The lobby (below) had an inviting stone fireplace and areas for comfortable lounging. (Both, courtesy of Bill McCutcheon.)

Streams of day-trippers took the trolley up Catoctin Mountain to enjoy respite from the summer heat in the cool air of Braddock Heights. Here, handsomely dressed travelers disembark from the trolley and walk or take a carriage ride up to the observatory (in the distance) and other attractions. (Courtesy of the Rhoderick family.)

The 1909 season was highlighted by the opening of the new Casino building, which featured a skating rink and a bowling alley. Summer crowds were treated to professional skating exhibitions and were offered the opportunity to win prizes at special events. The managers installed steam heating to enable the facility to remain open through the winter, and businessmen were encouraged in a newspaper advertisement to take an hour from their work schedules to "drive dull care away, invigorate you and make you more fit when you return to your duties." (Courtesy of Bill McCutcheon.)

The new Casino's top attraction seemed to be the roller rink. Guests could take lessons from the rink's professional skater or just enjoy rolling along to the music of a mechanical steam organ. In later years, the rink became the first in Maryland to use a plastic coating to protect the surface from excessive wear. Vacationers or day-trippers could also test their skills at the bowling alley in the basement of the Casino and, in later years, at the arcade on the same floor. The new facility replaced the alley that had previously been at the dance pavilion. (Both, courtesy of Sherry Kemp.)

In the 1940s, the roller rink became a year-round facility. In addition to skating, the building was used for dances (right), contests, and other special events. The roller rink vehicle below was a familiar site to Middletown Valley and Frederick residents. As Braddock Heights declined as an amusement park in the second half of the 20th century, the roller rink became the only amusement-related structure left from the park's heyday. Sadly, it was destroyed by fire in 1998. (Right, courtesy of Middletown Valley Historical Society; below, courtesy of Braddock Heights Historical Society.)

ROLLER SKATING & SOCK-HOP

JOHN STAUB

BRADDOCK HEIGHTS

ROLLER RINK

OVER $200.00 IN PRIZES

MEET YOUR FAVORITE DISC JOCKEY FROM

WMHI

BRADDOCK HEIGHTS, MARYLAND

FREDERICK COUNTY'S NEWEST STATION

FREE COKE Through the Courtesy of Frederick Coco-Cola Bottling Co.

FRAN LITTLE

FREE 2 TRANSISTOR RADIOS $24.95 VALUE

Through The Courtesy of Frederick Camera Shop

GENE SMITH

FRI. MAY 5th SKATING 7 P. M. to 9:30 Sock-Hop 9:30 till Midnite

ADMISSION 60¢ FOR THE EVENING

LOCATION - U. S. 40-A 5 MILES WEST OF FREDERICK

Baltimore, Md.
August 23, 1927

Manager
Amusement Park
Braddock Heights, Md.

Dear Sir:

On August 14th. (Sunday afternoon) the undersign with family had lunch in your park and hurrying to get things in car on account of rain my mother left her lower set of teeth behind, she remembers having them wrapped in a handerchief on her lap when she got up to leave they dropped on ground.unnoticed. We were sitting at the table between the swing and the merry go round on left side facing the merry go round.

Hoping that you will find time to attend to this and advise me please and if there is any expense attached to this (I mean outside of postage I will be glad to reimburse you.

Thanking you in advance for your prompt attention, I am

Yours very truly,
Paul E. White

Park guests sometimes left things behind. In the letter at left, a 1927 visitor asks for help in locating his mother's misplaced lower set of teeth. The writer details the area where the loss took place and notes that the lost ivories were wrapped in a handkerchief. On another occasion, a patron—identified on his stationery as an architect and building contractor—asks for help in finding a bathing suit, a white jumper, blue trunks, and a white belt. To assist in the search, and in keeping with his profession, he includes a carefully drawn map with the approximate location of the loss marked by an "X." While no documentation exists to determine the fate of these specific communications, other records suggest that all such requests were determinedly acted upon. (Both, courtesy of Braddock Heights Historical Society.)

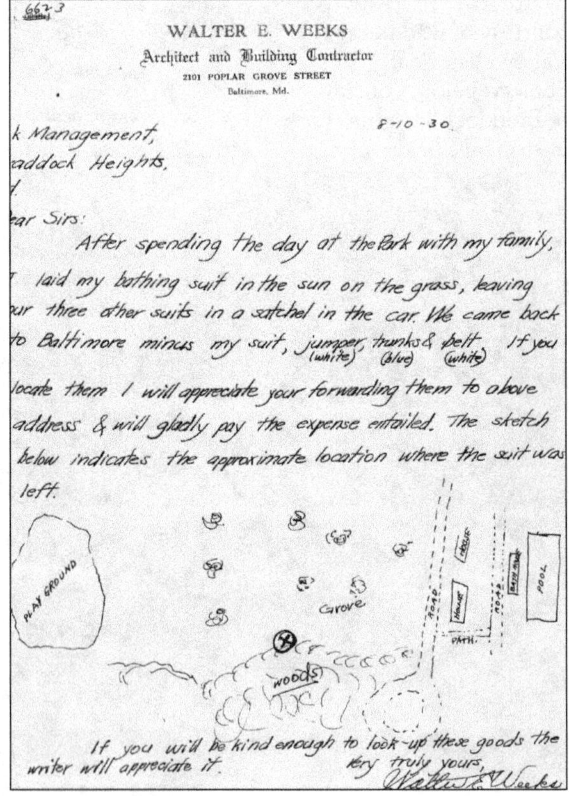

6623

WALTER E. WEEKS
Architect and Building Contractor
2101 POPLAR GROVE STREET
Baltimore, Md.

8-10-30

k Management,
raddock Heights,
d

ear Sirs:

After spending the day at the Park with my family, I laid my bathing suit in the sun on the grass, leaving our three other suits in a satchel in the car. We came back to Baltimore minus my suit, jumper (white), trunks (blue) & belt (white). If you locate them I will appreciate your forwarding them to above address & will gladly pay the expense entailed. The sketch below indicates the approximate location where the suit was left.

If you will be kind enough to look-up these goods the writer will appreciate it.

Very truly yours,
Walter E. Weeks

As Braddock Heights grew in popularity, large and sometimes grand homes and boardinghouses were constructed. One of the earliest residences, built by Thomas H. Myers in 1901, was the Avalon cottage. The following year, Myers added an annex with a large dining room, a bathroom, and 11 bedrooms. The Avalon was subsequently absorbed by the owners of the Valley View cottage. It was destroyed by fire in 1941. (Courtesy of Sherry Kemp.)

The Vindobona, originally a barn, was purchased in the early 1920s by George F. Wech, who added additional buildings and made it an inn. After a fire destroyed the structures in 1928, Wech rebuilt the hotel and, over time, added a number of buildings. The resort became a popular retreat for Washingtonians, including Pres. Franklin D. Roosevelt. The buildings were sold in 1954, and it became a nursing facility. (Courtesy of Vindobona Nursing & Rehabilitation Center.)

In 1906, the trolley line was extended from Braddock Heights to Jefferson. A new trolley station opened farther into the park on the route to Jefferson. It featured a snack bar and a post office in addition to an indoor waiting area. (Courtesy of Sherry Kemp.)

"Looking for a new place to take the entire family for picnicking and outdoor relaxation?" asked this post–World War II brochure. The answer: Braddock Heights Park, "high atop the beautiful Appalachian Mountains," with its swimming pool, Ferris wheels, merry-go-rounds, pony and boat rides, sliding board, miniature train, theater, roller rink, and bowling alleys. (Courtesy of Bill McCutcheon.)

Two

BURKITTSVILLE

In 1999, the tiny village of Burkittsville gained fame as the purported setting of the horror film *The Blair Witch Project*. The town, however, had witnessed true terror 137 years earlier.

On September 13, 1862, Confederate troops marched into Burkittsville and the surrounding area. Late the next morning, Union forces arrived in the area and engaged the southern army in fierce fighting through the streets of Burkittsville and the adjoining mountain gap. This action, part of the Battle of South Mountain, ended two days later at the Battle of Antietam, the bloodiest day of fighting in American history.

In the aftermath, the village became a virtual hospital. Later in the war, it saw additional troop movements. After the war, it reverted to its pastoral roots and life returned to its more traditional bucolic pace.

Burkittsville was only 37 years old at the outbreak of the Civil War. It began as a farming community and slowly grew to include shops, schools, churches, and small rural industries. In the 1880s, George Alfred Townsend, one of America's leading journalists and novelists, constructed an enormous estate on the mountain overlooking Burkittsville. Townsend had served as a newspaper correspondent during the Civil War and rediscovered the Middletown Valley while conducting research for a novel. His estate eventually encompassed 100 acres and included some 20 buildings. The crown jewel of the compound was an unusual monument constructed by Townsend to commemorate the service of war correspondents. The structure remains today, standing 50 feet high and 40 feet wide and including the names of 157 Civil War journalists, both Northern and Southern.

Burkittsville appears frozen in time. With the exception of a paved main street and a few nods to the contemporary world, the village could be cast as a Hollywood set for a nostalgic historical movie. Nearly the entire downtown area is listed in the National Register of Historic Places.

Burkittsville was established in the early 1800s at the crossroads of bisecting Indian trails, which became present-day Main Street and Route 17. The area west of Main Street was owned by Maj. Joshua Harley, who gave the town its first name, Harley's Post Office, in 1824. Henry Burkitt settled on the east side of Main Street and eventually became the town's namesake. By the time of the Civil War, the town had grown into a bustling community. During the Battle of South Mountain, Main Street was a conduit for troop movements in the area. Following the war, the town reclaimed its role as a small residential and commercial center amidst the surrounding agricultural area. Both of these images show Main Street, looking east (above) and west (below) in the late 1800s. (Both, courtesy of South Mountain Heritage Society.)

Henry Burkitt, one of the two founders of Burkittsville, built this home on his 160-acre farm in 1807 and lived in it until he died in 1836. The house was sold, and Burkitt's wife, Elizabeth, moved to the nearby stone home that Burkitt had built to house his slaves. It is said that on September 9, 1862, five Confederate cavalry officers took over the house, allowing the Burkitt family to remain in one section. When the Union army moved into town, the Burkitt family, their slaves, and the women of the town prepared food for the troops and, after the nearby battles, fed injured soldiers at the hospitals in Burkittsville. The large barn on the Burkitt property (below) was one of the buildings used as a hospital. (Both, courtesy of Wayne and Pat Guyton.)

The calm of this quiet village was violently interrupted on September 14, 1862, when Union forces marched through Main Street. At the western end of town, they confronted Confederate troops defending the road that crossed South Mountain at Crampton's Gap. The Northern army greatly outnumbered the Southern combatants, and by evening, Northern troops had broken through. However, darkness prevented the Union forces from taking advantage of their victory and crossing over the mountain. The delay, along with action elsewhere along South Mountain, culminated the following day in the bloodiest encounter ever fought on US soil: the Battle of Antietam. (Image from *Harper's Weekly*, October 25, 1862, courtesy of Library of Congress.)

In 1861, twenty-year-old George Alfred Townsend, whose pen name was Gath, became the youngest Civil War correspondent. He went on to great success as a journalist, novelist, and lecturer. In 1885, he purchased land at the top of South Mountain at the site of Crampton's Gap and designed an unusual, elaborate set of buildings as a summer estate for his family and guests. (Courtesy of Western Maryland Room, Washington County Free Library.)

Townsend constructed Gapland Hall, the main residential building, in 1885. He later added an L-shaped extension, and the home eventually contained 11 rooms. It was partially restored in 1958. Nearby was Gapland Lodge, which was built about the same time as the hall to house servants. Townsend used local stones in the creation of Gapland Hall. (Courtesy of South Mountain Heritage Society.)

At the crest of South Mountain at Crampton's Gap stands a unique and imposing monument created by Townsend to honor his fellow Civil War correspondents. This neo-Gothic structure was constructed in 1896 (above) and stands 50 feet high and 40 feet wide. It lists the names of over 150 correspondents, artists, and photographers from both the Union and Confederacy. Some of the stones in the monument were transported from Civil War battlefields. Maryland governor Lloyd Townes dedicated the War Correspondents Arch in October 1896, and Townsend deeded it to the War Department in 1904. In 1946, the monument's honorees were expanded to include war correspondents from all wars. In the photograph below, the monument is seen with other buildings of Townsend's estate, Gapland, in the background. (Both, courtesy of Western Maryland Room, Washington County Free Library.)

Townsend reportedly conceived of the design of the War Correspondents Arch while sitting on a train in a depot in Hagerstown, Maryland. He spotted the nearby Antietam Fire Company building and was moved to model his monument after its facade. "Gath" embellished his structure with busts of Greek gods, terra-cotta horse heads, and tributary quotes. In the image below, an adventurous visitor climbs the arch in the early 1900s to get an unauthorized closer look. (Right, courtesy of Western Maryland Room, Washington County Free Library; below, courtesy of McLuckie Collection, Maryland Room, Frederick County Public Library.)

The Resurrection Reformed Church was built in 1829, five years after Burkittsville's founding. It was jointly built and used by German Reformed and Lutheran congregations and called the Union Church until nearby St. Paul's Lutheran Church was constructed in 1859. Following the battle at Crampton's Gap, the building was used as a hospital. The church ceased operating as a house of worship in 1979. (Courtesy of South Mountain Heritage Society.)

In 1859, Burkittsville's Lutherans sold their interest in the Union Church and constructed St. Paul's. The edifice's tall steeple is a landmark in the area. The smaller steepled building is the former Lutheran school. St. Paul's was used as a hospital following the Battle of South Mountain. It has been said that President Lincoln visited wounded soldiers here on his trip to Sharpsburg after the Battle of Antietam. (Courtesy of South Mountain Heritage Society.)

Burkittsville, Maryland,
Sept, 18th 1862

Mr Cornelius Phillips.

Sir. it becomes my painfull duty to inform you of the Death of your Brother George, he received a wound at the storming of "Crampton Gap". wich cause his Death this morning, at 9 O'Clock. it was his wish that I should be with him so I staid by him till he died, he received his Death wound while doing his duty, and he died like a brave man. everything was done that could be done to make his last moments as comfortable as possible he died very easy and without pain, his last words were "Jim, fix me as you think I shall be the easiest". he was decently buried. I procured a headboard and marked his name on, he died in the German Reformed Church, of this Village, and he is buried about two hundred yards in the rear of the church, I cut of a lock of his hair wich I enclose in this letter, sympathising with you in your affliction I remain

yours Respectfully

James Denton

In its role as a Civil War hospital after the battle at Crampton's Gap, the Reformed Church saw much suffering and tragedy. In this poignant letter, Cornelius Phillips is informed of the death of his brother George at the church. "It was his wish that I should be with him," writes the deceased soldier's friend, "so I staid with him till he died." The writer assures Cornelius that George "died very easy and without pain" and was "decently buried" behind the church. As a keepsake, he encloses a lock of George's hair. (Courtesy of South Mountain Heritage Society.)

The Brethren congregation in the Burkittsville area was organized in 1776 and met in members' homes and barns until this church building was constructed in 1879. The original name agreed upon by the founders was Broad Run Church, after the settlement in Lancaster County, Pennsylvania, from which they had migrated to Maryland. Inspired by the extraordinary scene surrounding the newly built church, the congregation renamed itself Pleasant View. (Courtesy of Brethren Historical Library and Archives.)

Each summer, beginning in 1916, churches in the southern Middletown Valley joined together to hold outdoor Sunday evening services at the George Alfred Townsend estate grounds at Crampton's Gap. The sunset services began at 6:00 p.m. and often drew as many as 1,000 congregants, as it did here in 1926. (Courtesy of Brethren Historical Library and Archives.)

Burkittsville has had three public school buildings. There also was a school for African American children near the Ceres African Methodist Episcopal Church on the road to Crampton's Gap. Above, students are assembled outside the Burkittsville school, next to St. Paul's Lutheran Church, in 1897. In 1904, a new school was built in the eastern part of town. That building was destroyed by fire in 1913 and replaced the following year by the modern, fireproof school below. The new four-classroom building featured indoor plumbing, separate bathrooms for girls and boys, forced hot-air heating, and a basement play room and cloak room. Burkittsville's children were transferred to a new school in nearby Jefferson in 1968, and the Burkittsville school became a community center operated by the Ruritan Club. (Above, courtesy of South Mountain Heritage Society; below, courtesy of Jody Brumage.)

The largest structure in town was built in 1866 to house the Burkittsville Female Seminary. The school was established by the Lutheran church and, in the words of historian J. Thomas Scharf, taught "all the branches essential to a practical and ornamental education." The school operated until the last few years of the 1800s. (Courtesy of South Mountain Heritage Society.)

This home on Main Street was originally owned by Joseph Ennis and subsequently owned by his son William Ennis. William later purchased Needwood, the estate of Maryland's second governor, Thomas Sim Lee. The Burkitt family bought the home from Ennis and later sold it to the McBride family, seen here in the late 1800s. (Courtesy of South Mountain Heritage Society.)

US mail delivery to Burkittsville began in 1824. Pastor and historian H. Austin Cooper wrote that by 1829, the mail was being carried by the Stokes and Stockton Stage Coach Company. The route went between Baltimore, Maryland, and Staunton, Virginia, via Frederick and Shepherdstown. In Burkittsville, mail was dropped at the C.H. Biser stage stop, seen here in 1880. (Courtesy of Brethren Historical Library and Archives.)

Members of the Rohrback family have populated nearby Locust Valley since the mid-1800s. In this photograph, Edgar and Esta Rohrback relax with their grandchild on the porch of their two-story log home. The building was purchased in 1916 and included a one-story kitchen on the back. (Courtesy of Jody Brumage.)

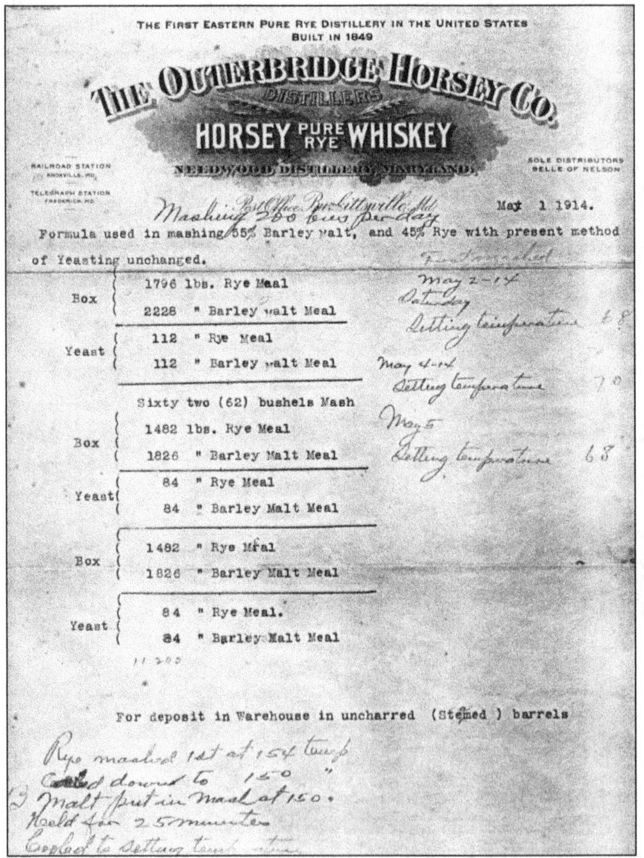

THE FIRST EASTERN PURE RYE DISTILLERY IN THE UNITED STATES
BUILT IN 1849

THE OUTERBRIDGE HORSEY CO.
DISTILLERS
HORSEY PURE RYE WHISKEY
NEEDWOOD DISTILLERY, MARYLAND.

RAILROAD STATION
TELEGRAPH STATION

SOLE DISTRIBUTORS
BELLE OF NELSON

Post Office Burkittsville Md.

Mashing 200 bus per day

May 1 1914.

Formula used in mashing 55% Barley malt, and 45% Rye with present method of Yeasting unchanged.

Box { 1796 lbs. Rye Meal
2228 " Barley malt Meal

Yeast { 112 " Rye Meal
112 " Barley malt Meal

Sixty two (62) bushels Mash

Box { 1482 lbs. Rye Meal
1826 " Barley Malt Meal

Yeast { 84 " Rye Meal
84 " Barley Malt Meal

Box { 1482 " Rye Mfal
1826 " Barley Malt Meal

Yeast { 84 " Rye Meal.
84 " Barley Malt Meal

May 2-14
Saturday
Setting temperature 68

May 4-14
Setting temperature 70

May 5
Setting temperature 68

For deposit in Warehouse in uncharred (Stemed) barrels

Rye mashed 1st at 154 temp
Cooled down to 150 "
Malt put in mash at 150.
Held for 25 minutes
Cooled to setting tank

The rye whiskey produced by the Outerbridge Horsey Distillery achieved fame far beyond the Burkittsville area. The company, formed in 1849, used an aging process that involved a sea voyage around the Cape of Good Hope to California and, several years later, a return trip to the distillery for production. The Outerbridge Horsey Company produced only one type of whiskey and sold enough of it to support the construction of a grand family estate (above). The ruins of the distillery are in the upper left of the photograph. During the Civil War, Confederate troops burned the distillery but, as the story goes, not before consuming enough of the spirits to significantly diminish their combat abilities. The formula for producing this beguiling brew is outlined in the 1914 document at left. The enactment of Prohibition in 1920 ended the Outerbridge Horsey Company's reign. (Both, courtesy of Richard and Pat Pry.)

Three

Harmony and Ellerton

In late 1780, as the Revolutionary War was about to enter its sixth and final year, Frederick City was the scene of an unusual encounter. A Tory spy mistakenly delivered a message to a Continental Army officer outlining a treasonous plot to free imprisoned British soldiers. The leaders of the conspiracy were gathered in the small village of Beallsville, some 10 miles from Frederick. The rural calm of the town was shattered as a squad of American soldiers arrested seven men and foiled the plot.

That small community recovered from its notoriety and a century later changed its name to Harmony, when, upon being granted its first post office, it was learned that another Beallsville, Maryland, already existed. By that time, the village had grown into a self-sufficient community with a variety of services, including general stores, a blacksmith shop, a shoemaker, and several mills. Churches and a school served the religious and educational needs of the bustling little village and the surrounding area was dotted with farms and green hills.

A well-trod dirt road led north from Harmony to the crest of a long hill where travelers came upon a magnificent view of the northern Middletown Valley. The tiny village of Ellerton lay at the bottom of the hill, about five miles from Harmony. This community grew up along a bubbling creek and was bisected by a busy road from Myersville to Wolfsville. As with other small Middletown Valley communities, the rural setting and the difficulty of transportation encouraged self-sufficiency. Through the years, Ellerton was served by two stores, a creamery, a blacksmith, a shoemaker, and other small enterprises.

Today, the old dirt road between Harmony and Ellerton has been paved, along with most of the other tracks in the area. The commercial establishments are long gone, and "outsiders" have built some modern homes. But many of the old houses and farms remain, and the rural feel is still very evident. And the view from the crest of the hill between Harmony and Ellerton continues to refresh the soul.

This panoramic photograph was taken from a hill south of Harmony. The Reformed Church, whose building later became the Harmony Band Hall, is in the center of the photograph, above and to the left of the former woolen factory, which was later the Leatherman store and the Ford store. (Courtesy of the Wisner family.)

This building in the center of Harmony was originally a gristmill and was then a woolen factory in the 1800s. William Brandenburg purchased it near the end of the 1800s and transformed it into a residence and general store. It has also housed the Harmony Post Office and a radio and television repair shop. The building was the site of the Revolutionary War treason incident described in the introduction to this chapter. (Courtesy of the Wisner family.)

Calvin T.K. Gladhill, the founder of Middletown's Gladhill Furniture Company, lived in Harmony before moving to Myersville after he married. In this 1890s photograph, he sits astride a horse in front of his home. Standing next to him are his mother, Magdalene, and his sister, Annie. (Courtesy of John C. Gladhill.)

Early German settlers to the area generally constructed log homes ranging in size from one story to four. Above is an example of a large, four-story cabin constructed of hand-hewn chestnut logs in the early 1800s. The kitchen/cooking area was on the ground floor, living areas were on the second and third floors, and an attic was on the top floor. (Author's collection.)

The Harmony Cornet Band was formed in 1916 with 12 members. Its founding officers were Charles Summers, Leslie Brandenburg, George Brandenburg, and Clarence Waters. The band grew in size and popularity and has continued into the 21st century, using the old Reformed Church in Harmony as its practice hall. In this early photograph, the band is assembled in front of the old Harmony schoolhouse. (Courtesy of John C. Gladhill.)

A spring or summer weekend was not complete without cheering on Harmony's baseball team in the Heart of Maryland League. Amateur adult baseball leagues were very popular in the first half of the 20th century, and most towns, large or small, fielded a community team. This photograph was taken at Harmony's home field: Gaver's meadow, near the area known as "the commons" and the town's crossroads. (Courtesy of the *Maryland Cracker Barrel.*)

In the early 1900s, apples were a major crop in the area. Apple trees covered the west side of Harmony, and Edward Gaver processed the fruit at his cider press on Hollow Road, across the bridge from "downtown." (Courtesy of the Wisner family.)

Potatoes were also an important crop on many farms in the Harmony area. Area residents often engaged in "truck farming," growing what they could on smaller properties and trucking them to market to earn extra cash. James Baker of Harmony displays some of his yield in this family photograph. (Courtesy of the Wisner family.)

Ann Maria Moser was a daughter of Daniel Leatherman, one of the earliest Brethren settlers in the Middletown Valley. In 1802, she designed her home near Harmony (above) so that the first floor could be used for religious services, which were held in the home until 1837, when work began on a new church 100 yards below the house. The new church, called the Ann Maria Moser Church, was completed in 1840 and served the community until the Civil War. The present Harmony Church of the Brethren was built in 1870 and incorporated some of the logs from the Ann Maria Moser Church. The building originally had two front doors (below), one for women and one for men, as the two genders sat separately for services. (Both, courtesy of Mary Specht.)

The Baker family of Harmony is descended from early settler Daniel Leatherman and his daughter Ann Maria Moser. In 1926, the extended family—125 people—held a reunion at the Ezra Baker home in Harmony. Baker, the great-grandson of Daniel Leatherman, was a principal builder of the Beallsville (later Harmony) Church of the Brethren and the founder of the first Sunday school. (Courtesy of Mary Specht.)

The Harmony Lutheran Church was constructed in 1879 to serve local congregants who had been traveling to Middletown or Myersville for services. For many years after the church was built, a pastor from the neighboring Lutheran church visited Harmony to lead services, often on Thursday evenings. In 1989, the church became independent of the Zion Lutheran Church in Middletown and hired its own pastor. (Courtesy of Carroll Leatherman.)

During the Great Depression, one of Pres. Franklin D. Roosevelt's New Deal agencies, the Works Progress Administration (WPA), performed roadwork in the crossroads area of Harmony. In this home snapshot, note the WPA sign at the right and the Harmony Lutheran Church at the left. (Courtesy of the Wisner family.)

Local farmers assisted in the modernizing of the main road through Harmony by loading their wagons with large rocks from their farms and delivering them to downtown Harmony. The large machine seen here would crush the stones for use on the new road. (Courtesy of Evelyn Haynes.)

Harmony's early public school was a brick, two-story structure (above) across from Harmony Lutheran Church. It was replaced by a wooden building at the same location (below). A fire during the 1921–1922 school year destroyed the school, but it was quickly rebuilt. The school closed in 1938, and Harmony's children were sent to the Myersville elementary school. One of the most memorable teachers in the Harmony school was Robert Ridgley, who rode his horse to school from his home in Myersville. Ridgley was a stern disciplinarian who was known to the adults in the community as a teetotaler, searching out illegal stills during Prohibition and alerting Internal Revenue agents about their locations. (Above, courtesy of Carroll Leatherman; below, courtesy of the Wisner family.)

The Thomas F. Bittle store (above) was the hub of Ellerton for many years. The building was constructed in the late 1860s and sold feed, shoes, clothing, hardware, candy, and other general goods. It also housed the community's post office. Bittle expanded into the undertaking business in 1884. According to local historians Charles Martin and Tom Rose, Bittle did not allow cards or music in the store, but he did permit well-behaved loafers to linger and debate the issues of the day. After Bittle's death in 1917, his son J. Thomas Bittle took over operation of the businesses. The store closed in 1950. The receipt below was from an 1889 purchase of wholesale grocery goods by Thomas F. Bittle from a Frederick dealer. (Above, courtesy of the Charles S. Martin family; below, courtesy of Arthur Leatherman.)

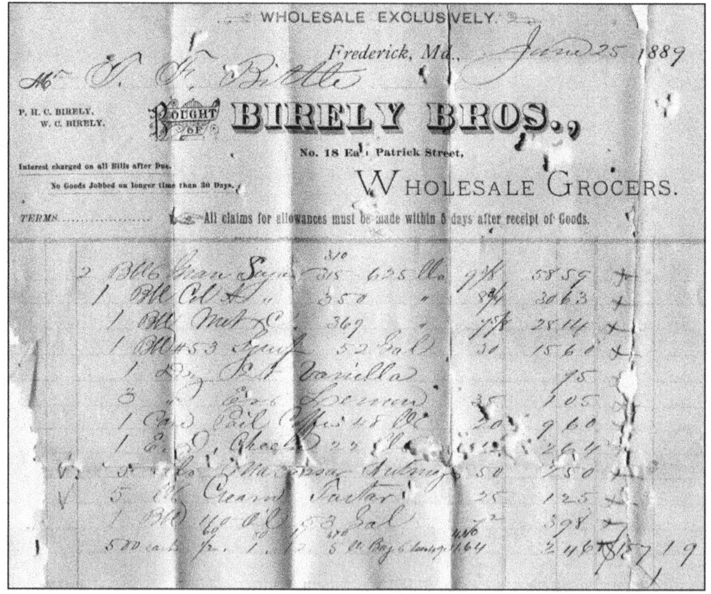

WHOLESALE EXCLUSIVELY.

Frederick, Md., June 25 1889

Mr T. F. Bittle

P. H. C. BIRELY.
W. C. BIRELY.

Bought of BIRELY BROS.,

No. 18 East Patrick Street,

WHOLESALE GROCERS.

Interest charged on all Bills after Due.

No Goods Jobbed on longer time than 30 Days.

TERMS........ All claims for allowances must be made within 6 days after receipt of Goods.

An old advertisement from the Bittle store outlines some of the medical remedies it offered for sale. The Chamberlain Medicine Company, based in Des Moines, Iowa, was a producer and purveyor of a large line of products sold throughout the country in the early 1900s. Seen in this Bittle store notice, Chamberlain's product line covered a wide variety of ailments. (Courtesy of Arthur Leatherman.)

WE SELL

Chamberlain's Cough Remedy, famous for its cures of bad colds and as a preventive and cure for Croup, 50 cents per bottle.

Chamberlain's Pain Balm, a general family liniment and especially valuable for rheumatism, sprains, bruises, burns and frost bites, 50 cents per bottle.

Chamberlain's Colic, Cholera and Diarrhœa Remedy the most successful medicine in use for dysentery, diarrhœa, colic and cholera morbus, 25 and 50 cent bottles.

St. Patrick's Pills. They are the best physic. They also regulate the liver and bowels.

Try them, 25cents per box.

Chamberlain's Eye and Skin Ointment for tetter, salt-rheum, scaldhead, eczema and chronic sore eyes. 25 cents per box.

In addition to the Bittle store, tiny Ellerton was served by the Summers general store. John F. Summers purchased the business from Washington Gaver in 1882, and the store remained in the Summers family until it closed in 1971. Note the gentleman lounging on the sofa at the side of the store. (Courtesy of the Charles S. Martin family.)

The first Grossnickle Church of the Brethren, between Ellerton and Middlepoint, was a log structure built in 1847. It was replaced in 1899 by the present large brick building. The spacious attic, now the site of the Sunday school, accommodated the traditional Love Feast and Communion gatherings. It was divided into sections for male and female members. (Courtesy of Grossnickle Church of the Brethren.)

Peter Grossnickle played a leading role in building the Grossnickle Church. His son Elias, seen here holding the bible, purchased this farm from his father and passed it along to his son C. Upton Grossnickle (standing, fifth from left). Upton was one of the organizers of the Flook, Gaver, Leatherman, Summers, and Grossnickle Bank of Myersville. (Courtesy of Wayne and Karen Grossnickle.)

The Ellerton School (above) stood near the road connecting Myersville and Wolfsville, opposite Middle Creek. It was constructed in the early 1870s and remained in operation until the late 1920s. Harvey Grossnickle, the principal and instructor for a number of years in the early 1900s, kept a ledger (below) in which he meticulously entered details regarding attendance, books, and facilities at the school. At the bottom of each page, he made extensive notations about the day's weather. (Both, courtesy of Anna Mae Doub.)

Register of Public School No. 7, Election District No. 6,

Months. April May

NAMES	Miles from School	Age Last Birthday	Date of Entrance	Date of Withdrawal	1st Week Weekly Attendance	2d Week Weekly Attendance	3d Week Weekly Attendance	4th Week Weekly Attendance	5th Week Weekly Attendance	6th Week Weekly Attendance	7th Week Weekly Attendance
Teacher, H. R. Grossnickle					0	4	5	5	5	5	5
1st Assistant, Clifford Bittle		14	4/16		0	4	5	5	5	5	5
2d Assistant, Silas Bittle		13	"		0	2	2	5	2	2	4
Foster Grossnickle		12	"		0	3	4	5	5	5	5
Hubert Harp		11	"		0	1	2	3	3	0	1
Harry Baker		9	"		0	4	5	5	5	4	5
Ralph Harshman		11	"		0	4	0	0	4	2	5
Geo. Grossnickle		10	"		0	4	4	3	1	3	3
Wilbur Summers		9	"	5/20	0	4		5	5	4	5
Elmer Leatherman		11	"	4/20	0	0	0	0	0	0	0
Samuel Routzahn		10	"		0	4	5	5	4	4	
Elmer Johnson		9	"		0	3	5	5	5	5	
Elmer Shepley		10	"		0	4	5	5	5	5	
Orvalle Shepley		8	"		0	3	3	3	0	3	

Apple trees in full bloom

One way to cool off on a hot summer's day in the Ellerton area was to load the family in the buggy and take a ride over to Highland Falls (above). This popular picnic spot was on private property, but it drew crowds of visitors on sunny days. Near the falls is a large overhanging rock, which, according to archeological studies, was used by Native Americans around 2000 BC as sleeping quarters and as a sitting space during inclement weather. The shelter area was originally 30 feet wide, but road construction cut it back to the size seen below. Older residents sometimes referred to the shelter as "Hog Rock" because a former owner used it as an enclosure for pigs. A prehistoric rhyolite boulder field bordering the shelter was used by early Native Americans as a quarry. (Above, author's collection; below, courtesy of Babs Savitt.)

Four

Middletown

The weather was sunny and beautiful on September 13, 1862. William Pickerall was crossing Catoctin Mountain with the 3rd Indiana Cavalry on the way to what would be several days of bloody carnage. Yet writing later in his journal, Pickerall was moved to describe the pacific scene that greeted him at the crest of the mountain. "Encircled with forest crowned mountain ranges, I have seen no lovelier landscapes than the Middletown Valley."

The town he encountered at the base of the valley that day was a thriving community, surrounded by lush farmland. Middletown had been established nearly 100 years earlier and had grown to become a commercial and residential center. Its population was composed largely of members of its four principal religions: United Brethren, Lutheran, German Reformed, and Methodist Episcopal. In addition to shops, homes, and churches, the town boasted a newspaper, tanneries, boardinghouses, and a location astride the National Road.

In addition to the troop movements and the nearby Battles of South Mountain and Antietam, Middletown's Civil War experiences included a frightening threat of destruction averted by the payment of a ransom to Confederate forces. Over the next three decades, the town settled back into its role as the bustling center of the surrounding agricultural community. In 1896, Middletown's horizons broadened considerably when the electric railway line from Frederick was extended to a depot at the eastern edge of town. The railway soon reached Myersville and later Hagerstown. The town entered a period of expansion, with homes and businesses sprouting around the trolley routes. Writing in 1925, the publisher of the weekly *Middletown Valley Register* boasted that the town's homes were among the finest in Maryland, noting that, "All the sidewalks of the town are of concrete, the streets are lighted with electric lights, and, in fact, it is a modern and up-to-date town."

Through the ensuing years, the town has remained "up-to-date," as it and the surrounding area have attracted increasing population and commercial growth. Yet the downtown area of Middletown today looks much like it did a century ago, and the community has retained its small-town atmosphere.

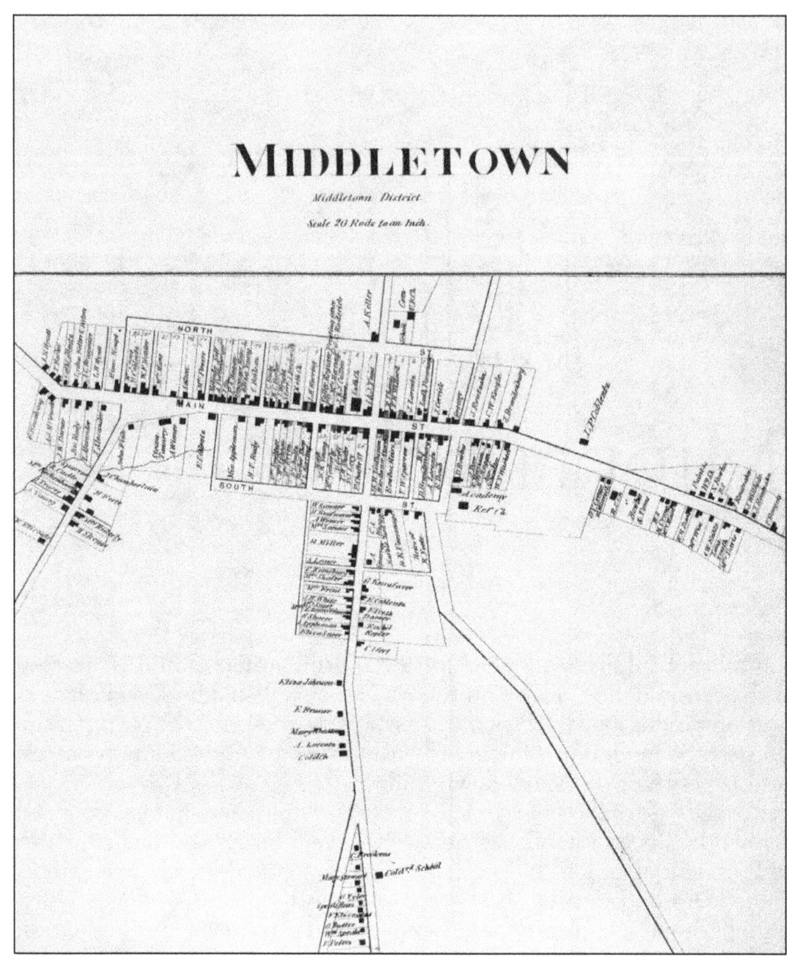

When the Civil War finally ended, Middletown resumed its role as a commercial and residential center for the surrounding agricultural community. The map at left, from the 1873 Titus Atlas of Frederick County, shows the National Road, Middletown's Main Street, as it passed through the town. Matching the map with the 1872 photograph below, there were homes, shops, and churches along this stretch of West Main Street. The steepled buildings are the Lutheran parsonage, in the foreground, and the Zion Lutheran Church. (Both, courtesy of the Rhoderick family.)

The lush green of summer in the Middletown Valley often contrasted with frosty white when winter storms rolled in. A blizzard in 1895 buried Middletown in several feet of snow. The above photograph was taken on Jefferson Street. The building on the left is the African AME Church. The storm made travel through town along the National Road extremely difficult. In the photograph below, West Main Street is still covered in snow after a period of cleanup. The building behind the oval sign on the left is the old City Hotel. (Both, courtesy of the Rhoderick family.)

The small building at left in the above photograph, constructed in 1880, began its life as Kepler's Harness Shop and was subsequently a tailoring shop, a jewelry store, a millinery business, and a barbershop. In 1896, Thaddeus Hauver, the principal of the Middletown Public School, built the large structure on the right in the photograph to house his growing stove and tin business as well as his family. For several years after Hauver's death, at age 42 in 1898, the store remained a stove shop and then served as a post office and a confectionery (below) under proprietor Melanchton Gaver. In its latter incarnation, men of the town gathered there regularly in the evenings to loaf. (Both, courtesy of the Rhoderick family.)

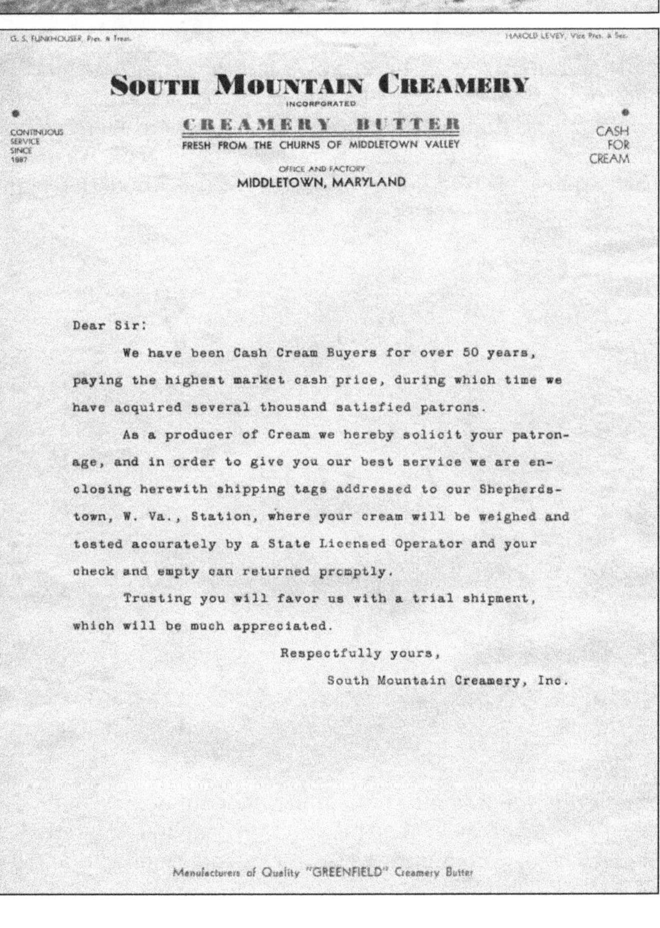

G. S. FUNKHOUSER, Pres. & Treas. HAROLD LEVEY, Vice Pres. & Sec.

SOUTH MOUNTAIN CREAMERY

INCORPORATED

CONTINUOUS SERVICE SINCE 1887

CREAMERY BUTTER

FRESH FROM THE CHURNS OF MIDDLETOWN VALLEY

CASH FOR CREAM

OFFICE AND FACTORY

MIDDLETOWN, MARYLAND

Dear Sir:

We have been Cash Cream Buyers for over 50 years, paying the highest market cash price, during which time we have acquired several thousand satisfied patrons.

As a producer of Cream we hereby solicit your patronage, and in order to give you our best service we are enclosing herewith shipping tags addressed to our Shepherdstown, W. Va., Station, where your cream will be weighed and tested accurately by a State Licensed Operator and your check and empty can returned promptly.

Trusting you will favor us with a trial shipment, which will be much appreciated.

Respectfully yours,

South Mountain Creamery, Inc.

Manufacturers of Quality "GREENFIELD" Creamery Butter

The Shank Creamery was owned by brothers John and Martin Shank when, in 1888, their younger brother Charles left the family farm in Myersville to serve as manager. In 1897, Charles became a half-owner of the thriving business, and 11 years later, he purchased the entire operation. As a leading businessman in Middletown, he was a director of the Valley Savings Bank and played a major role in the promotion and construction of Middletown's Memorial Hall. The Shank Creamery became the South Mountain Creamery (above, in 1914) as Charles continued to modernize the plant. He originated a butter-renovating process and dealt in a variety of products. The operation expanded to other locations and, as seen at right, was a major buyer of cream from area farms. (Both, courtesy of Middletown Valley Historical Society.)

Old Joe Lorentz, seen here, was a familiar figure around Middletown in the 1890s, hauling buttermilk from the Shank Creamery to local customers. This photograph of Main Street shows, from left to right, the front porch of the Edward Herring home, Mrs. Herring's millinery shop, the H.S. Stephens tailoring shop (later the Eugene Alexander barbershop), and the Charles L. Gaver shoe store and home. (Courtesy of the Rhoderick family.)

Spoolsville was a small, rural, industrial community about one mile west of Middletown. Adam Koogle set up a wagon shop next to his home in the late 1840s and owned the property until the late 1890s. The community also included a flour mill and a blacksmith shop. (Courtesy of the Rhoderick family.)

"Hoggin' time" in the Middletown Valley, as elsewhere, was an occasion for families and friends to turn farm-raised pigs into food for the coming months. Everyone pitched in and, after the work was done, gathered for a hearty meal and well-earned social time. The John Hanson family gathered for this photograph during hoggin' time on their farm. Below, the menfolk of an unidentified family in the South Mountain area make the first cut. (Above, courtesy of Middletown Valley Historical Society; below, courtesy of Doug Bast.)

William C. Dillon posed proudly with his bicycle in this 1885 photograph outside his home—the old Adam Koogle farmhouse—on the National Road just west of Middletown. Dillon grew up in Middletown, married, and settled in Spoolsville, just outside of Middletown, where he worked as a wagon maker. He fell victim to the worldwide influenza epidemic and died in 1918. (Courtesy of the Rhoderick family.)

An area outside of Middletown known as "Picnic Woods" was the scene of many outdoor gatherings from spring to autumn. A Middletown community picnic was an annual highlight and, as seen in this photograph, drew hundreds of participants dressed in their Sunday finery. (Courtesy of the Rhoderick family.)

Dr. Austin Lamar, the son of a Wolfsville doctor, set up his own practice in Middletown in 1900. He was deeply involved in town life and served as burgess of Middletown between 1912 and 1913. In 1905, he purchased a property on Main Street and, over the next few years, expanded it into a full-service hospital (above). The announcement of the grand opening in the *Valley Register* (below) noted that the new sanitarium was a "modernly equipped Hospital for the cure and treatment of all Acute and Chronic Diseases that are non-contagious as well as Surgical and Obstetrical Cases." The three-story medical center had 21 rooms, including offices, a reception area, a library, a dining hall, a kitchen, and bedrooms. (Above, courtesy of Middletown Valley Historical Society; below, author's collection.)

DR. A. A. LAMAR'S SANITARIUM

MIDDLETOWN, MD.

Open to the Profession and Public, Jan. 4th, 1908.

A modernly equipped Hospital for the cure and treatment of all Acute and Chronic Diseases that are non-contagious, as well as Surgical and Obstetrical Cases.

Facilities and Equipment Unsurpassed

For the Proper Execution and Affter Treatment of all Surgical Affections

Physicians have absolute contro of the ir patients.
All rooms strictly private.
Special trained, Graduate or Training School Nurses, provided.
Our rates as low as the most scientific treatment and the best nurs ing will permit.

For further information, write or telephone.

C. & P. Phone No 5 — **Dr A A LAMAR,**
Md. Phone No. 352—6 — **Middletown, Md**

The Zion Lutheran Church on Main Street was preceded in that location by two structures, a log church built in the 1770s and the brick church that replaced it in 1814. The present building, seen at left in 1921, was built in 1859. At various times in their histories, the Middletown Lutheran and Reformed congregations shared a building. During the Civil War, the Lutheran Church, like its counterparts, served as a hospital, with pews covered by wooden planks or torn out to make room for cots. The church was reimbursed for damages after the war. In 1928, the congregants added a Sunday school chapel. Seventeen years later, as World War II was drawing to a close, the church celebrated the final payment for the chapel with a mortgage-burning ceremony (below). (Left, courtesy of the Rhoderick family; below, courtesy of Middletown Valley Historical Society.)

RALLY DAY

MORTGAGE BURNING CELEBRATION

OCTOBER 7, 1945

Dear Members and Friends of Zion Church:—

At last the great day, so long looked for by all of us, is to be a reality. We are going to burn the final Mortgage of $2,176 at the Service on Rally Day, and then the Sunday School Chapel will be debt free.

Of course, we will need the Rally Day Offering to make this possible, and every loyal member and friend of Zion Church and Sunday School should have a financial as well as spiritual part. If at all possible each one should be present to make a contribution and to share in the joys of the Day; and those who cannot be present should have a part in the final Mortgage Burning by sending a contribution to Miss Anna Dinterman, marked "Rally Day Offering."

The Sunday School session will begin at 9:30 o'clock and then at 10:00 o'clock we will go, in a body, into the Sanctuary for the Mortgage Burning Ceremony and to hear an address by Dr. A. R. Wentz, president of Gettysburg Seminary.

IF AT ALL POSSIBLE

Be Present

IF YOU CANNOT BE PRESENT

Send Your Contribution

Faithfully yours,

The Finance Committee

In 1798, Conrad Crone, the developer of Middletown and a member of the Lutheran Church, conveyed a small parcel of land on the corner of Jefferson and Washington Streets to the church's trustees for construction of a parsonage. The Parson's House (above) was sold in 1848, when a new brick parsonage was completed on Main Street (below, in 1914). A separate two-story lecture hall next to the new building was used for a female academy, operated by the church. Students were educated in two departments: "Juvenile," where young ladies learned "the rudiments of an English education . . . such as Spelling, Reading, Defining, etc." and "Academic," where they were taught "Penmanship, English Grammar, Geography, History, Mathematics, the Natural and Moral Sciences, Mental Philosophy, the Ancient and Modern Languages, and Music." (Both, courtesy of the Rhoderick family.)

In the late 1700s, the German Reformed residents of the Middletown area constructed a log church in the vicinity of what is now Church Street. The present brick structure was built in 1818.The congregation ran into serious financial difficulties during its first decade in the new building and had no permanent minister. Rev. J.C. Bucher of Cavetown took charge of the Middletown church and is credited with saving it from dissolution. Prior to the Battle of South Mountain, Union general George McClellan reportedly viewed the battlefield terrain from the church's belfry. A 16-foot addition to the church was built in 1889, and in 1902, a Sunday school chapel was added. In the above image, several boys play on the fence in front of the Reformed Church in 1896. The church's sanctuary is seen below, also around 1896. (Courtesy of the Rhoderick family.)

For 69 years beginning in 1829, free African American residents of Middletown worshipped at the Asbury African Methodist Episcopal Church on Jefferson Street. Burials in the adjoining graveyard continued until 1927. The cemetery and parts of the church's foundation survived a fire in the late 1950s. In 2001, the Middletown Valley Historical Society, Middletown Scouts, and other local groups rededicated the cemetery. (Courtesy of Middletown Valley Historical Society.)

The Brethren Church at the corner of Main and Church Streets was built in 1882. It was called the Otterbein Chapel after Philip William Otterbein, the founder of the United Brethren in Christ Church. When the Evangelical United Brethren Church merged with the Methodist Church in 1968 to form the United Methodist Church, the congregation continued to use the Main Street location until moving to a new United Methodist building in 1978. (Courtesy of the Rhoderick family.)

Early Methodist Episcopal congregations in Middletown shared a building with members of the United Brethren Church. This structure (left) was built in 1831 and was referred to as the Martin Box because of its birdhouse-like look. It was located on present-day Green Street in what is now the Lutheran Cemetery. The Methodist Episcopal congregation built its own church on Main Street (below) in 1853. The church's membership eventually declined, and the building was sold in 1919. It has been used over the years as a library, an auxiliary school building, and finally as an apartment house called the Wesleyan Apartments. (Both, courtesy of the Rhoderick family.)

The citizens of Middletown had watched thousands of Confederate troops march through their town during the second week of September 1862. On September 13, the blue-clad Union army appeared on Main Street in pursuit of the Southern forces. In this drawing from *Harper's Weekly* magazine, Union troops head towards fateful battles at South Mountain and Antietam. (Courtesy of Library of Congress.)

The farm of Daniel Wise near Fox's Gap was the scene of an enduring historical controversy when the corpses of 58 Confederate soldiers were discovered in a well on the property. Wise allegedly contracted with the Union army to bury the fallen men and then disposed of them in his well. Twelve years later, the bodies were moved to graves at the Confederate Cemetery in Hagerstown. (Courtesy of the Rhoderick family.)

At the Battle of South Mountain, a 40-year-old Ohio lawyer, Lt. Col. Rutherford B. Hayes (left), was severely wounded and taken to the home of Jacob Rudy on Main Street in Middletown (below). He recovered, was wounded several more times during the war, and rose to the rank of brevet major general. Hayes was elected to Congress in 1864 while still in military service, but he refused to take office until the war ended. He was elected governor of Ohio in 1867. In 1876, after a disputed national election, Hayes became the 19th president of the United States. During his term, he oversaw the controversial end of the Reconstruction era, enacted civil-service reforms, and instituted a variety of measures to strengthen business and industry. (Left, courtesy of Library of Congress; below, courtesy of Middletown Valley Historical Society.)

Head Qar: Valley Dept
July 8 1864
The contribution of five thousand
dollars ($5000.) levied upon the
town of Middletown commuted
to ($1500) fifteen hundred dollars
to be paid by the town authorities
by 7 o clock tomorrow morning
The remainder of the amount
($3500) thirty five hundred dollars
must be paid by the township
or Election district of Middleto
by six o clock tomorrow afternoon

By order of
Lt-Genl Early

A S Pendleton
Lt-col & a a g

In July 1864, Confederate forces under Gen. Jubal Early rode into Middletown on an incursion aimed at Washington, DC. On behalf of General Early, commanding officer Lt. Col. A.S. Pendleton demanded a ransom of $5,000 from town leaders in exchange for sparing the town from fiery destruction. Burgess William J. Irving argued that he could not raise such a large amount immediately and convinced Pendleton to accept an initial $1,500, with the remaining $3,500 to be paid later in the day. Pressed for time to rejoin the main army near Frederick, the Confederate contingent left Middletown before collecting the remainder of the ransom. (Courtesy of Middletown Valley Historical Society.)

In the late 1800s, one-room schools were established in the small communities around Middletown. The days and hours of operation were often dictated by agricultural seasons and family responsibilities. Many children trudged miles to attend classes. At left, teacher Alvey Beachley stands at the far left with his charges at the Everhart School, outside of Middletown. Below, students at the Mount Tabor School gather in the doorway of their building. (Both, courtesy of the Rhoderick family.)

Two schools were established in Middletown after the Civil War, operating in the Lutheran and Reformed Church lecture rooms. Shortly afterward, civic leaders formed the Middletown Classical Academy for more advanced studies. These included Latin, Greek, general science, mathematics, English, and German. The teacher, William Avis, was reputed to be a strict scholar who demanded that entering students have a relatively strong educational background. Middletown's first public school was built in 1881 on West Green Street and was celebrated with a gala grand opening, seen here. In its early years, the school served elementary students and used only two of its four rooms. (Courtesy of the Rhoderick family.)

Middletown's high school classes were held at Grangers' Hall from 1888 to 1894, when the Frederick County Board of Education purchased the old Catholic church on East Main Street. The building had been constructed in 1868, but the declining Catholic population in Middletown led to its closing. This photograph shows principal C.E. Dryden's high school class in the mid-1890s. (Courtesy of the Rhoderick family.)

In 1864, during Confederate general Jubal Early's incursion into the Middletown Valley, the bridge over the Catoctin Creek was burned down. It was soon replaced with a new covered bridge (above). Nearly 60 years later, in 1923, an automobile crash claimed two lives and seriously damaged the bridge. The old covered span was torn down and replaced with a concrete structure. (Courtesy of the Rhoderick family.)

The building of the electric railway from Frederick to the Middletown Valley in 1896 proved to be a welcome gateway to the 20th century for local farmers and citizens. The deteriorating condition of the National Road and the expense of building a railroad over the sparsely populated mountains between Frederick and Hagerstown had left the area with a poor transportation system. Local newspapers closely followed the progress of construction and residents eagerly anticipated the commencement of service. Construction of trestles across the hills and dales of the route (right) posed a challenge, but, as seen below, the structures were completed successfully. (Both, courtesy of the Rhoderick family.)

The electric railway station in Middletown was at the eastern end of town, a half-mile from the center of town at the top of a hill. After much grumbling from townspeople, a station was built near the center of Middletown on what is now Green Street. (Courtesy of the Rhoderick family.)

This photograph was taken from the belfry of the Reformed Church around 1900. South Mountain is in the distance, and Main Street, marked by the spires of the Zion Lutheran Church and the Methodist Episcopal Church, runs horizontally across the scene. (Courtesy of Middletown Valley Historical Society.)

Middletown's Main Street was decked out in finery for the Boosters' Festival and Home Coming Week in 1914 (above). The *Frederick News* reported that "600 electric lights have been installed to form a court of honor" on Main Street. Events during the week included downtown concerts each evening, educational presentations, box suppers, entertainment for children, speeches, athletic events, and a large parade. Maryland governor Phillips Lee Goldsborough and former governor Edwin Warfield gave special addresses on the final day of the celebration. Visitors driving to Middletown along the National Road were greeted by painted advertisements like the ones below, touting the products of Main's Ice Cream shop and the Valley Stove House. (Both, courtesy of Doug Bast.)

After a fire destroyed the Middletown public school on Green Street in 1907, a new school to house all grades (above) was built on Prospect Street. Discipline among high school boys was a problem in the combined school, according to a history written by Harry M. Gross. Principal R.E. Kieney, described as "an excellent instructor" and "master of the art of discipline," remedied the situation. In later years, as the area's population grew, an additional building was constructed for the high school, seen below in 1935. (Above, courtesy of Middletown Valley Historical Society; below, courtesy of the Draper family.)

The entire student body of Middletown High School gathered outside the front entrance of the building in 1915 for the group photograph above. Then, as now, graduations were occasions for both solemnity and celebration. The four-page commencement program for the class of 1922 indicates that a total of 11 musical performances were presented, along with the pastoral invocation and benediction and the commencement address. No students spoke at the ceremonies. The class yell, motto, flower, and colors were printed on the final page (right), along with the list of graduates and class officers. (Both, courtesy of Middletown Valley Historical Society.)

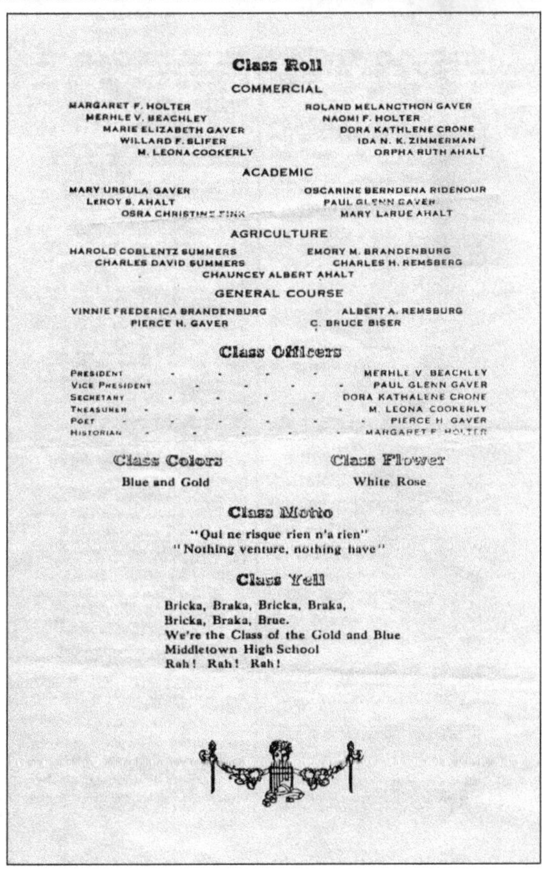

Class Roll

COMMERCIAL

MARGARET F. HOLTER
MERHLE V. BEACHLEY
MARIE ELIZABETH GAVER
WILLARD F. SLIFER
M. LEONA COOKERLY
ROLAND MELANCTHON GAVER
NAOMI F. HOLTER
DORA KATHLENE CRONE
IDA N. K. ZIMMERMAN
ORPHA RUTH AHALT

ACADEMIC

MARY URSULA GAVER
LEROY S. AHALT
OSRA CHRISTINE FINK
OSCARINE BERNDENA RIDENOUR
PAUL GLENN GAVER
MARY LARUE AHALT

AGRICULTURE

HAROLD COBLENTZ SUMMERS
CHARLES DAVID SUMMERS
EMORY M. BRANDENBURG
CHARLES H. REMSBERG
CHAUNCEY ALBERT AHALT

GENERAL COURSE

VINNIE FREDERICA BRANDENBURG
PIERCE H. GAVER
ALBERT A. REMSBURG
C. BRUCE BISER

Class Officers

PRESIDENT	MERHLE V. BEACHLEY
VICE PRESIDENT	PAUL GLENN GAVER
SECRETARY	DORA KATHALENE CRONE
TREASURER	M. LEONA COOKERLY
POET	PIERCE H. GAVER
HISTORIAN	MARGARET F. HOLTER

Class Colors

Blue and Gold

Class Flower

White Rose

Class Motto

"Qui ne risque rien n'a rien"
"Nothing venture, nothing have"

Class Yell

Bricka, Braka, Bricka, Braka,
Bricka, Braka, Brue.
We're the Class of the Gold and Blue
Middletown High School
Rah! Rah! Rah!

For five generations, the major newspaper of the Middletown Valley was largely run by the Rhoderick family. Mahlon Rhoderick partnered with H. L. Brady to purchase the weekly Catoctin Whig in 1844. Rhoderick's nine-year-old son George Carlton Rhoderick was an employee. The paper became the *Valley Register* and, in 1858, George became sole owner. He published it continuously for the next 48 years, with the exception of one week in 1862 when Confederate forces occupied Middletown. His son, George Carlton Rhoderick, Jr. (left) began working at the newspaper office at the age of 14 and became owner when his father died in 1906. His son, George Carlton Rhoderick III (below), took over when George Jr. died in 1924 and continued the family tradition of deep civic involvement while running the newspaper and printing business. (Both, courtesy of the Rhoderick family)

Beginning in 1845, the *Catoctin Whig*, and subsequently the *Valley Register*, was published in a small building on West Main Street. In 1870, George Rhoderick Jr. moved the building to the rear of the lot and erected a new structure (right) for his newspaper. The *Valley Register* and the printing business remained in the Rhoderick family, in the same building, until 1984, when it was sold to John Saxon. George Rhoderick IV, the great-great-grandson of Mahlon Rhoderick, maintained an active role in the newspaper's publication. The newspaper ceased operation in 1991 after covering events great and small for a century and a half. Below, the end of World War I is described on the front page. (Right, courtesy of Middletown Valley Historical Society; below, author's collection.)

Established 1844 Sworn Circulation 2356

The Valley Register.

A Family Newspaper Devoted to Literature Local & General News

VOLUME 75 — MIDDLETOWN, MARYLAND, NOVEMBER 15, 1918 — NUMBER 23

THE WAR OVER; ARMISTICE SIGNED

Armistice Signed at 5 O'clock Monday Morning at Foch's Headquarters—Fighting Ceased at 11—Everything for Which America Fought Has Been Accomplished, Says President Wilson

PANDEMONIUM REIGNED IN EVERY CITY AND TOWN

It is Estimated That 10,000,000 Lives Have Been Lost in Over Four Years of Bloody Struggle as a Result of Germany's Thirst for World Domination—The Kaiser a Fugitive in Holland—Four Rulers of the Central Powers Dethroned—President Wilson's Proclamation

$1,000 SHORT OF GOING "OVER THE TOP"

Middletown District Running Behind in the United War Work Drive—Only $1,700 Subscribed So Far—Come Forward and Back Up Our Boys—They Deserve it

SYNOD OF POTOMAC MEETS NEXT MONDAY

Forty-sixth Annual Session Will Convene in Christ Reformed Church, Middletown—Cantata to Be Rendered Tuesday Evening—Interesting Program Arranged

PEACE JUBILEE NEXT MONDAY AT FREDERICK

Three Aeroplanes Will Give a Wonderful Exhibition of Flying—Monster Parade Starts at 2 O'clock, With 8 Bands—Every District Should Be Represented

HOW MIDDLETOWN CELEBRATED THE END OF THE GREAT WAR

Bells Rang and Whistles Blew One Hour and Half From 4 O'clock Monday Morning

THE KAISER'S FUNERAL HELD MONDAY EVENING

Big Parade Escorts the Hearse Drawn by Two Mules—Town Officials Act as Pall-Bearers—Band and Singers in Line With Many Decorated Automobiles and Floats—Whole Town Beautifully Decorated—Services Held in Reformed Church After Parade

Emory L. Coblentz embodied the modern term "multitasker." The son of a Middletown farmer, Coblentz began his post–high school life as the assistant treasurer of Middletown's Valley Savings Bank when it was formed in 1887. While there, he studied law and, in 1898, left the bank to begin his own practice. Coblentz somehow found time to help organize and lead the Frederick Electric Railway Company and the Potomac Edison Company. He was also president of the Central National Bank and the People's Fire Insurance Company as well as a director of the Maryland Brick and Supply Company, the Braddock Heights Water Company, and the Braddock Heights Building and Development Company. Coblentz also served in the Maryland House of Delegates and in the Maryland State Senate. During the Great Depression, his Central Bank failed and he lost a significant amount of his personal wealth attempting to keep the institution afloat. Coblentz died of cancer in 1941. (Author's collection.)

Virtually every Middletown Valley community fielded a band or two. These groups practiced regularly and performed at local civic and church functions. The highlight for many band members was performing in area parades. In the 1894 photograph at right, the American Band marches in Middletown's annual Fireman's Parade. The march was part of a full day of festivities sponsored by the Middletown volunteer fire department. The photograph below shows a crowd of citizens gathered during the festival at the creamery at the west end of town. (Both, courtesy of the Rhoderick family.)

The Model Garage, established in 1915 on West Main Street, served as Middletown's all-purpose automobile center. "Autoists" could purchase gasoline, get their vehicle repaired or serviced, and replace tires. Behind the Main Street facility, the garage had a showroom where prospective buyers could examine vehicles for sale. As seen below, drivers had to be cautious when entering and driving through the town limits of Middletown; speeds over eight miles per hour were prohibited. (Above, courtesy of the Rhoderick family; below, courtesy of McLuckie Collection, Maryland Room, Frederick County Public Library.)

Many of Middletown's buildings housed multiple establishments over the years. This building was erected in 1790 as a residence but, over the years, was occupied by a doctor's office, Middletown's first telephone exchange, a confectionery, an insurance company, and, for a brief time in 1908–1909, it was the temporary home of the Middletown Savings Bank. (Courtesy of the Rhoderick family.)

The accompanying cut shows a picture of the building which I recently purchased and where I will soon locate my store. I will have on hand a full line of DRY GOODS, GROCERIES, QUEENSWARE, HARDWARE, OILS, PAINTS and GENERAL MERCHANDISE. Also SCHOOL SUPPLIES. ¶Thanking you for past favors, and hoping for a continuance of same, I am, very respectfully,

GEORGE L. DOUB, Middletown, Md.

In 1914, George L. Doub purchased a property on an alley off Main Street and announced that he was in the process of establishing a full-line general store. Doub had been burgess of Middletown from 1910 to 1912 and served in that office three more times in the 1920s and 1930s. (Courtesy of Middletown Valley Historical Society.)

STATE THEATRE

MIDDLETOWN, MARYLAND

SHOWS AT 7 AND 9 P. M. — "MAKE A DATE WITH THE STATE"

Theatre Open Wednesdays, Thursdays, Fridays and Saturday — "Always the Best Entertainment Possible"

CASH NIGHT EVERY WEDNESDAY NIGHT

This Calendar and One Regular Admission Will Admit Two Persons To This Theatre On Feb. 25, 1943

1943 FEBRUARY 1943

WED	THUR	FRI	SAT
3 TOPICAL THRILLS! EXCITING ACTION! Preston Foster and Brenda Joyce in "LITTLE TOKYO, U. S. A" ALSO—Comedy, Cartoon CASH DRAWING 9 P. M.	**4** HERE IT IS! Comedy, Romance, Grace and Beauty in a Wonderland on Ice! Sonja Henie, John Payne and Jack Oakie in "ICELAND" ALSO—Short Subject Friday Night—Chapter 8, "Captain Midnight"	**5**	**6** Those Bums— The Brooklyn Dodgers in a baseball mystery "It Happened In Flatbush" Lloyd Nolan, Carole Landis ALSO—Comedy, Cartoon, Latest News and Chap. 8, "Captain Midnight"
10 Comedian Red Skelton in "Panama Hattie" with Ann Sothern and Marsha Hunt ALSO—Comedy, Short Subject CASH DRAWING 9 P. M.	**11** The Stars of "Honky Tonk" Together Again!! Clark Gable and Lana Turner in "Somewhere I'll Find You" ALSO—Cartoon Friday Night—Chapter 9, "Captain Midnight"	**12**	**13** Here's Western Thrills! Lloyd Nolan, Donna Reed and William Lundigan in "Apache Trail" ALSO—Latest News, Cartoon and Chapter 9, "Captain Midnight"
17 Cary Grant, Jean Arthur and Ronald Colman in "Talk of the Town" ALSO—Comedy, Short Subject CASH DRAWING 9 P. M.	**18** HERE'S LAUGHS GALORE! Mickey Rooney in "A Yank At Eton" with Freddie Bartholomew and Tina Thayer ALSO—Selected Short Subjects Friday Night—Chapter 10, "Captain Midnight"	**19**	**20** "Blondie For Victory" with Penny Singleton, Arthur Lake, Larry Simms, Daisy ALSO—Comedy, Cartoon, Latest News and Chap. 10, "Captain Midnight"
24 DOUBLE FEATURE! James Craig, Pamela Blake in "Omaha Trail" Plus: Jinx Falkenburg and Russell Hayden in "Lucky Legs" CASH DRAWING 9 P. M.	**25** STAND BY! for the Year's Greatest Action-Packed Story of the Sky! Pat O'Brien, Evelyn Keyes and Glenn Ford in "FLIGHT LIEUTENANT" ALSO—Comedy and Short Subject Friday Night—Chapter 11, "Captain Midnight"	**26**	**27** Joe E. Brown at his comical best in "The Daring Young Man" ALSO—Latest News, Cartoon and Chapter 11, "Captain Midnight"

Coming Soon . . To your theatre . . For your enjoyment

Marjorie Main in "TISH"

Judy Garland and Gene Kelly in the hit of the season, "FOR ME AND MY GAL"

Van Heflin in "SEVEN SWEETHEARTS"

After the conclusion of World War I, two local businessmen—Emory Coblenz, president of the electric railway company, and Charles Shank, owner of the South Mountain Creamery—proposed the construction of a community hall in memory of Middletown Valley's fallen military servicemen. When completed in 1923, the building housed a theater for movies and stage shows, meeting rooms, a kitchen, and a large community room (above). Coblenz and Shank donated half of the $55,000 cost, the local American Legion post assumed responsibility for funding the theater, and the Middletown community raised the money for the remainder of the bill. The building was a popular community center used for a variety of activities. In later years, the auditorium became the State Theatre, featuring the Hollywood movies of the day (left). (Both, courtesy of Middletown Valley Historical Society.)

YES! 1914.

I know you are a busy chap. You have only a year to live, but you must carry my message to all the people in this section. Whisper in their ear about the things they need, and tell them to buy them of the man who can be met every day.

You and I are at home here. We like the Country and we are all Booster's for this section. Handing you out an article in exchange for cash is not the whole thing. The salt of success is Loyalty, Friendship, and Helpfulness. Make this store your headquarters for Home Coming week, and don't have the feeling that you must buy when you come in this store. Take it easy, look around, make it a place for studying Quality, Prices, and Things that last and suit.

I can supply you with goods to build and preserve your homes; I will help to spread your table with good things; also can furnish you with Xmas., Wedding, or Birthday gifts, and you will get good values for your money.

The best in the beginning is always the cheapest in the end, and I want to at this point assure all my patrons of my gratefulness to them, many of whom have been customers of this store since 1887.

L. Z. DERR

MIDDLETOWN, - - MARYLAND.

One of Middletown's largest and most enduring commercial establishments was the L.Z. Derr general store. Constructed in 1892, the handsome building's second floor was the home of the proprietor, Luther Derr, and his family. The *Valley Register* described the new building in detail and opined, "Middletown has too few such enterprising citizens as Mr. Derr, and unfortunately there are too many who are trying to pull down instead of building up the town." Derr ran the business until his death in 1918 and was succeeded by his son L. Osmond Derr, who operated it until he died in 1963. This clever, chummy advertisement was printed in the program book for the 1914 Middletown Boosters' Festival and Home Coming Week. (Courtesy of Middletown Valley Historical Society.)

In the late 1920s, Mr. and Mrs. Charles Rhoderick established the Yellow Tea Room on Main Street. The building dated back to the early 1850s and through the years had been occupied as a residence, a confectionery, a clothing store, a harness shop, a shoe repair shop, and an insurance office. (Courtesy of the Rhoderick family.)

Middletown's first apartment house was owned and operated by Adam W. Smith on the second floor of his general store on Main Street. Smith also ran a carriage business in the rear of his property. When he relocated to Lincoln, Nebraska, in 1890, Smith held a public sale that drew the large crowd seen here. The building housed a tavern in Middletown's early days. (Courtesy of the Rhoderick family.)

Like many of its contemporaries in the 1800s and early 1900s, the Gladhill Furniture House also offered undertaking and embalming services. In the above photograph, local youths enjoy a mock ride on the Gladhill funeral wagon. Below, proprietor Calvin T.K. Gladhill and assistant Danny Harp enjoy an afternoon respite on the front porch of the furniture store's showroom. The business was launched in 1908 when Gladhill and his wife, Lola, sold some of the furniture in their Myersville home to an admiring visitor. Soon afterward, they opened a furniture store in their barn. Their inventory grew to include home furnishings, cookstoves, jewelry, and carriages. In 1915, the Gladhills purchased the Schlosser Tannery on Walnut Street in Middletown and relocated the business. The undertaking business was sold in 1980, and the store was sold in 1998. (Both, courtesy of John C. Gladhill.)

Middletown had a number of hotels for travelers along the National Road and on the electric railway line. One of the oldest hotels was located on West Main Street and dated back to at least the 1840s. At various times in its history, it was called Galt House, City Hotel, Valley House, Hotel Gaver, and Valley Hotel (seen here in 1914). (Courtesy of Middletown Valley Historical Society.)

Travelers could also stay at one of the town's boardinghouses. The Shafer House, seen here, was located off Main Street and boasted "all modern conveniences," including electricity and two bathrooms to serve the occupants of its 14 rooms. In the early 1940s, another Main Street boardinghouse, the Maples, offered "all corner rooms" and "good beds with coil springs and innerspring mattresses" at a cost of 50¢ to 75¢ per night. (Courtesy of Middletown Valley Historical Society.)

In the years following the Civil War, baseball grew in popularity and became America's national pastime. Town teams were formed in communities throughout the Middletown Valley and they became a source of civic pride and heated rivalry. A Middletown High School team was formed soon after the school's establishment; the 1911–1912 squad is seen above. The school later produced a major professional baseball star, Charlie "King Kong" Keller (right). After graduating from the University of Maryland, Keller joined the New York Yankees in 1939 as a left fielder alongside Joe DiMaggio. He played for 13 seasons and compiled a .286 batting average, with 189 home runs. After retiring, he established the Yankeeland horse farm and owned a gas station in Middletown. His brother Hal Keller also played professional baseball. (Above, courtesy of Middletown Valley Historical Society; right, courtesy of Dwight Hutchinson.)

One of Middletown's most popular commercial establishments for most of the 20th century was Main's Ice Cream shop. Charles F. Main (above), the son of a farmer, opened a butchering business in Middletown in 1892 at the age of 22. The meat store was on Main Street and the slaughterhouse was on nearby Jefferson Street. Main built an icehouse behind the store and was patronized by local homeowners needing to stock their iceboxes. He soon expanded his business to include the sale of ice cream and created a number of flavors using locally grown fruit. As noted in the 1914 advertisement below, "Once Used, Always a Customer." The long lines outside the shop on hot summer days attested to the veracity of the advertisement. (Above, courtesy of Jane Main Young; below, courtesy of Middletown Valley Historical Society.)

ICE CREAM

ICE CREAM ICE CREAM

All Flavors. Any Time

All the Time.

Once Used, Always a Customer.

C. F. MAIN

Phone 110. MIDDLETOWN, MD.

ICE CREAM

Five

MYERSVILLE

Like the other towns of the Middletown Valley, Myersville was settled by earnest folks who focused their lives on hard work and religion. But according to Ira Moser, who ran the local newspaper in the early 1900s and wrote a history of Myersville, a grog shop was established in a stable in town in the mid-1800s. "This place was the scene of the most disgraceful conduct, brawls, etc. every night, especially on Saturday nights." It was called the "old lick," and it operated for a number of years. Other such establishments sprang up, "and gambling was carried on in these shops." A magistrate ran one of the grog shops and "sold the liquor one day and fined his customer on the next."

Such carrying on came to an end in 1864, when Upton Buhrman, an influential local citizen-politician, was able to muster support for an ordinance banning the sale of intoxicating liquor within three miles of the churches of Myersville.

The village returned to its role as a small and quiet rural community for several decades until the outside world literally rolled in. On an autumn day in 1898, an electric railway car lurched into Myersville, connecting it with Middletown and Frederick and forever changing life in the little town. It was then possible to ship locally grown produce to more distant locations.

Two banks and several additional commercial establishments opened in town, and in 1904, when trolley service was extended to Hagerstown, Myersville became an incorporated community. New, modern homes were built in town along with a brick school to consolidate the student bodies of the local one-room schools.

Despite its broadened role, the town's population of several hundred remained relatively steady through the first half of the 20th century. Following World War II, a new road passing within yards of downtown Myersville offered travelers a way to avoid the scenic but twisting old National Road. The subsequent growth has altered the landscape to a moderate extent, but the town and its environs remain "country" in look and feel.

Myersville was a relatively isolated community of 200 as the 19th century drew to a close. There were poor road connections to the area's two nearest cities, Frederick and Hagerstown, from which modern transportation was available to the rest of the nation. In 1898, a group of Myersville businessmen formed the Myersville and Catoctin Railway Company and raised the funds necessary to extend the trolley line from Middletown to Myersville. Construction (above) began in the spring and was completed in October. The Myersville railroad company then leased the line to the Frederick and Middletown Company for an annual five-percent return on its investment. The round-trip fare between Myersville and Middletown was set at 20¢, and the round-trip to Frederick was 50¢. The trolley tracks ran along Myersville's Main Street to the center of town (below). (Above, courtesy of the Charles S. Martin family; below, courtesy of Dick Phelps.)

In 1898, the year the trolley came to town, several local businessmen established Myersville's first bank. Its first board of directors met on the second floor of George Bittle's store and focused on serving local interests. The Myersville Savings Bank grew and expanded with the town, and in 1902, it moved into the handsome new quarters above. The bank survived the Depression, closing for only three days during President Roosevelt's mandated bank holiday in 1933. Several months after the Myersville Savings Bank opened, a second bank was established in the fast-growing town. Flook, Gaver & Co. also prospered and was reorganized in 1903 as The Banking Firm of Flook, Gaver, Leatherman, Summers, Grossnickle & Co. Its failure during the Great Depression affected many local residents and businesses. (Courtesy of Dick Phelps.)

Shortly after Myersville became an incorporated community in 1904, the members of the newly formed Corporation Council signed an agreement with the management of the Frederick and Hagerstown electric railways to facilitate the extension of the line west to Hagerstown. The council granted the railway companies permission to lay down track and run the trolley along the south part of Main Street. While a boon to Myersville, the agreement was backed by unfulfilled verbal promises that left the streets a mess during the first winter. The above photograph shows a muddy and rutted Main Street. In the photograph below, taken years later, downtown Myersville shares its Main Street equally between trolleys and motorcars. (Both, courtesy of Dick Phelps.)

As Myersville grew as a commercial center, two local cousins engaged in a bit of familial competition. George W. Bittle, the son of an Ellerton farmer and merchant, came to Myersville in 1891 and became the proprietor of the G.W. Bittle General Store (above). Eight years later, he helped establish the Myersville Savings Bank and became its treasurer. He was also appointed Myersville's postmaster during the presidential administrations of Benjamin Harrison and William McKinley. About a decade after Bittle arrived in Myersville, his cousin Lawson F. Bittle established a general store a short distance away on Main Street (below). The L.F. Bittle store housed the town post office for several years. Both establishments seemed to prosper. (Above, courtesy of Stanley Kline; below, courtesy of Dick Phelps.)

Office of the

Frederick County Guide,

AN INDEPENDENT WEEKLY PAPER.

Published Every Friday by D. H. Mowen.

LARGE CIRCULATION.

GOOD ADVERTISING MEDIUM.

Myersville, Md., July 5th 1896

C J Bittle 1 Topic book pd 5
W. R. & J. E. Moser 1 " " pd 5
Joseph Wolf 1 " " pd 5
S. W. Bittle 1 " " pd 5
Ira Moser 1 " " Pd 5
Easton A Smith 1 " " pd 5
William Wachter " " Pd 5
John Horine " " pd 5
Columbus Houpt " " pd 5
L. M. Koogle " " pd 5
R. S. Harp " " pd 5
Jule Wachter " " Pd 5
Effy J Hildebrand " " Pd 5
Saloma Smith " 5
Annie Poffenberger " Pd 5
Lizzie Poffenberger " Pd 5
William Harp " pd 5

John T. Hildebrand was a leading carriage maker in the northern Middletown Valley. He acquired the property for the home above on the south end of Main Street from his father-in-law, Joseph Brown, who operated Myersville's first post office in his downtown store. Soon after it was built, this handsome home was featured in Ira Moser's 1905 *History of Myersville*. (Courtesy of Ann Brown.)

Myersville's first newspaper, the weekly *Frederick County Guide*, was published at three different locations during its tenure, from 1891 to 1901. As with many newspaper operations of the time, the publishers also contracted to do printing jobs in the community. This image documents the 1896 sales of "topic books" to a number of customers, many of whom were prominent Myersville citizens. (Courtesy of St. Paul's Lutheran Church, Myersville.)

In 1901, Ira C. Moser (right) purchased the *Frederick County Guide* and changed its name to the *Myersville Monitor*. Moser, the son of a Myersville businessman and town councilman, was 20 years old when he acquired the newspaper. He set up shop on Main Street (below) and was a strong promoter of the town. In 1904, he joined with other town leaders to form the Business Men's Protective Association to encourage industries to locate in Myersville. The following year, he wrote and published a brief history of Myersville, extolling the virtues of "one of the most beautiful little towns in Maryland." (Right, courtesy of St. Paul's Lutheran Church, Myersville; below, courtesy of Kathy Falkenstein.)

These bird's-eye view photographs were taken soon after the electric railway began spurring development in Myersville. The above image looks south along Main Street. The roofs of the Rhoe and Blands Creamery are visible opposite the Lawson Bittle house and store. In the photograph below, taken from the belfry of the St. Paul's Lutheran Church on Main Street, the Flook, Gaver & Co. Bank stands in the foreground alongside the Farmers Mutual Exchange and the electric railway trolley barn. (Both, courtesy of Kurt Bittle.)

With the advent of trolley service, travelers seeking cool respite from summertime heat could more easily reach Myersville for day trips or extended stays. The Shank House on Main Street served as a hotel and boardinghouse from the late 1890s to the 1920s. (Courtesy of Kathy Falkenstein.)

The 1910 *History of Frederick County* described this home on Main Street as "a handsome two-story brick dwelling [with] a bank barn, and convenient outbuildings." It was owned by a bachelor, Wendall A. Smith, who was "prominent among the progressive young farmers of the district." Smith later married and was active in local Republican Party affairs. The home is near the site of the log cabin built by Myersville's earliest settler, James Stottlemyer. (Courtesy of Dick Phelps.)

Established 1844
Sworn
Circulation 2350

The Val

VOLUME 75 MIDDLETOWN,

$30,000 FIRE AT MYERSVILLE 5 BUSINESS PLACES BURNED

Disastrous Blaze In Sub-Station of H. & F. Railway, About 1.30 Last Saturday Afternoon.

CITIZENS STOOD BY POWERLESS--- NO FIRE PROTECTION IN THE TOWN

Trolley Car Barn, Sub-Station, Farmers Exchange Store, Central Trust Co. Bank and Elevator All Destroyed—Two Families Lose All Household Effects—All the Burned Structures Will Be Rebuilt—Farmers Exchange Heaviest Losers.

While the citizens of Myersville, this valley, stood by and looked on hopeless and powerless, fire which broke out in the sub-station of the Hagerstown & Frederick Railroad Company, shortly after 1 o'clock last Saturday afternoon, spread unfought and unchecked, until nearly $30,000 worth of valuable property had been destroyed.

The town has no fire protection, and nothing could be done to hold the flames in check. The sub-station, car barn, station and offices were all under one roof, and this whole structure was destroyed, with a loss of from $7,500 to $10,000.

From here the flames spread to the Farmers' Exchange, a 2-story frame building, 115 by 32 feet, filled with a valuable stock of goods in both store and cellar and with two families occupying the flats above. Loss on building, $7,500; on stock, about $7,000.

While this structure was wrapped in flames, the grain elevvator in the rear of the Farmers' Exchange, took fire and was consumed, with a loss of $2,500 on building, and $3,000 on contents.

The Myersville branch of the Central Trust Co. of Maryland, separated from the blazing inferno by only a four-foot alley, was next attacked. Although a brick structure with a slate roof, sparks quickly set fire to the southeast cornice, and the blaze ate its way under the roof and gutted the place. Notes, drafts, checks, currency, etc., were quickly shoved into the fire-proof vault by Mr. John Eldridge, assistant treasurer of the bank, and the building vacated. The loss here is about $1,500, fully covered by insurance.

The apartments of John W. Eldridge, assistant treasurer of the bank, and David Mock, over the store room, were burned, with a loss of a portion of their contents. Mr. Eldridge lost a piano that could not be removed. Mr.

$15,000 FIRE AT GAPLAND SAT. NIGHT

Hamilton Shafer's Grain Elevator and Contents, B. & O. Freight Warehouse, and Three Sheds Destroyed—Nearly 400 Bushels of Wheat Lost—Mr. Shafer Critically at the Time.

Fire at Gapland, along the Washington County Branch of the B. & O. Railroad, just over the Frederick county line from Burkittsville, this valley, shortly before 8 o'clock, destroyed the large grain elevator and contents, owned by Hamilton W. Shafer, of near Burkittsville, the B. & O. freight warehouse and three adjoining buildings owned by the railroad and a stable of Elmer L. Gordon, entailing a loss estimated at $15,000.

The grain shed contained 40 tons of mill feed, between 300 and 400 bushels of wheat, a carload of hay, a carload of cement, a carload of ground lime and a large quantity of corn, all of which were destroyed.

Sparks from the burning elevator soon started fires in the railroad freight warehouse, but not until all of the contents of this building had been removed. It further spread to the two warehouses owned by Mr. Shafer and adjoining the grain elevator and a wood shed, destroying these structures also.

The fire was discovered in the end of the grain elevator about ten minutes after the passenger train going to Hagerstown, had passed, this fact causing the belief that a spark from the engine might have been responsible for the fire. For a time it was thought that the entire settlement would be wiped out.

The entire community, disregarding the intense cold, turned out and battled the flames, forming a bucket brigade, the only means at hand to cope with the fire.

The elevator was the outlet for grain grown for many miles around Gapland, many growers even in Frederick county taking their grain to Gapland for shipment. It is estimated that between

On January 4, 1919, a devastating fire in downtown Myersville destroyed the trolley depot, Central Trust Bank, the Farmers Mutual Exchange, and nearby residences (above). At left, the *Valley Register* reported that the conflagration began in the trolley substation and spread rapidly to the surrounding area. With no means of fire protection in Myersville, officials and residents could do little to stop the flames. The town council had been debating the feasibility of developing a municipal water system but the expense was daunting. A volunteer fire company was organized in Myersville in 1925, but the town did not purchase its first fire engine until 1931. (Above, courtesy of the Charles S. Martin family; left, author's collection.)

The 1919 fire in downtown Myersville destroyed the building that housed the Farmers Mutual Exchange, a general store operated by Albert and Cyrus Flook. It was rebuilt, and in 1924, it was renamed the People's Supply Store by its new owners, Walter Falkenstein and Oliver Smouse. The business included a mill and warehouse behind the store. People's Supply was a particularly popular place for children, with its ice cream and soda fountain, and for men who enjoyed a traditional small-town loafing place. Note the elegant Doric columns in front of the store (above). In the early-1930s photograph below, the store's proprietors, Oliver Smouse (center) and Walter Falkenstein (right), tend to customer Tilghman Grossnickle (left). (Above, courtesy of Kathy Falkenstein; below, courtesy of the Charles S. Martin family.)

In 1905, the directors of the prospering Flook, Gaver & Co. Bank constructed what historian T.J.C. Williams described as "the best equipped banking building for a town the size of Myersville to be found in the state." This impressive structure was destroyed in the Myersville fire of 1919 but was soon rebuilt and consolidated with a large Frederick-based institution. The bank failed during the Great Depression and never reopened. (Courtesy of Dick Phelps.)

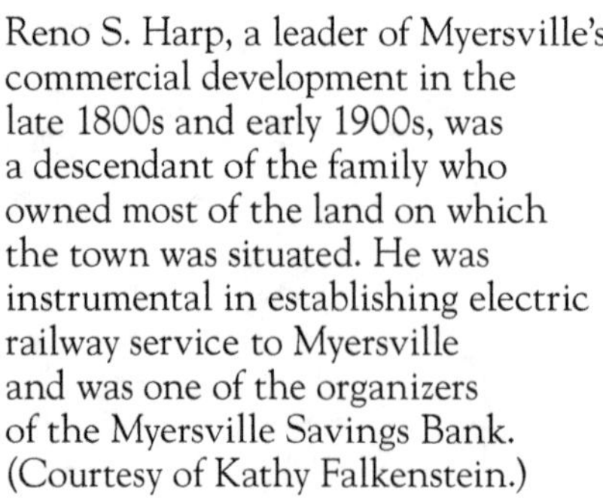

Reno S. Harp, a leader of Myersville's commercial development in the late 1800s and early 1900s, was a descendant of the family who owned most of the land on which the town was situated. He was instrumental in establishing electric railway service to Myersville and was one of the organizers of the Myersville Savings Bank. (Courtesy of Kathy Falkenstein.)

An automobile dealership opened across from the trolley depot in 1916. The Myersville Motor Company originally sold Hudson, Dodge, Willys-Overland, and Essex automobiles. The Rice brothers took over the business in 1920 and sold Willys-Knight and Overland vehicles (above). Wilbur Summers purchased the building in 1927, and for the next 30 years, he operated the garage and sold Desoto, Plymouth, Star, and Durant cars. At right, members of the Summers family and workers stand outside the entrance to the garage. After the Summers family sold the business, the building went through several transitions and served as a used car store and service garage, a convenience store, and a chocolate factory. (Both, courtesy of the Summers family.)

A ride on the electric railway from Myersville to Middletown took about 20 minutes and cost 10¢. Above, Car No. 160 leaves the terminal on Main Street for Middletown in 1941. It was built in Cincinnati in 1909 and contained seats for 40 people. Trolley cars were equipped with cowcatchers to protect against livestock wandering onto the tracks. Train conductors (below) worked long hours and were well known to passengers along the route. The car in the photograph below was affectionately known as "Old Mike." Trolley service in Myersville ceased in 1944. (Above, courtesy of Maryland Room, Frederick County Public Library; below, courtesy of Kurt Bittle.)

The first school in Myersville was a one-room building in Frog Hollow, a half-mile from town on what is now Monument Road. It was replaced in 1905 with the town's first brick school (above), on Main Street. This four-room school was steam-heated and served the community until it was replaced in 1927 with a new building on Harp Place (below). In 1971, a new elementary school was built, after which the school on Harp Place was used as a community center and town hall until it was demolished in 2010. (Both, courtesy of the Charles S. Martin family.)

It is generally agreed that the first settlement in the Middletown Valley was near Myersville and was called Jerusalem. This stone monument at left states that "the first churches of Western Maryland were built on or near this site" as early as 1711. While historical analysis casts serious doubt on that date, there is no question that the first religious settlement in the Middletown Valley occurred at the Jerusalem site. (Courtesy of Babs Savitt.)

The United Brethren in Christ settled and worshipped at Jerusalem in the early 1800s, sharing the church with their Evangelical Lutheran neighbors. In 1852, the Brethren community built a church in Myersville on the northern end of Main Street. A violent storm in 1891 so severely damaged the church that it had to be razed. Within a year, a new brick building was constructed. (Courtesy of Anna Mae Doub.)

After sharing the Jerusalem church for several years, the Lutheran congregation constructed a log church some two miles north of Myersville. This was replaced in 1830 by the present stone St. John's Evangelical Lutheran Church. It was part of the Middletown charge until its own charge was created in 1849. (Courtesy of Kathy Falkenstein.)

St. Paul's Evangelical Lutheran Church, on Main Street in Myersville, was originally part of the St. John's Church charge. The original building, erected in 1856, was destroyed by a fire that began in John Hildebrand's carriage shop in 1872. The present structure was completed the following year. A Moller pipe organ was added in 1896. (Courtesy of the Charles Martin family.)

The Myersville Church of the Brethren (above) was formed in 1913 to provide a local house of worship for the town's growing Brethren population. Many of the congregants were members of the Grossnickle Church who had moved into Myersville or its immediate vicinity. The *Valley Register* reported that the church's cornerstone was purchased in Schwartzenau, Germany, the town from which the American Dunkard Church founders emigrated. As was traditional, the church (below) was simple and sparsely furnished. Note the stove used for heating the building in cold weather. (Both, courtesy of Debbie Wilson.)

In July 1926, Myersville was the site of a gathering of 800 of George S. Harp's descendants. Harp (1765–1844) was one of the founders of the nearby St. John's Lutheran Church. When the present stone structure was built in 1830, Harp purchased the old log church and used the materials to construct a dwelling near Ellerton, which still stands. The 1926 reunion featured a full day of music, prayer, and lectures. The descendants included relatives with familiar Middletown Valley names such as Bittle, Grossnickle, Horine, Summers, Leatherman, Toms, Flook, Harshman, Wachtel, and many others. (Both, courtesy of the Summers family.)

The picturesque Eldridge farm, outside of Myersville, was built in 1808. In its over 200 years of existence, it has passed through a succession of families, including the Doubs, Routzahns, and Falkensteins. Its 170 acres have traditionally produced crops to feed its large herd of dairy cattle. (Courtesy of Kathy Falkenstein.)

Rural mail delivery began in the Myersville area in 1901. The first carrier was John M. Grossnickle, who used this horse-drawn vehicle on his rounds. True to the postal service's pledge, he delivered the mail in all weather conditions and was known for the many poems he penned about his work. (Courtesy of Kathy Falkenstein.)

Bittle was a well-known name in the Myersville-Harmony-Ellerton area. The photograph above was taken around 1895 on the home place of the John Henry "Hen" Bittle family on Bittle Road. "Hen" Bittle passed the farm along to his son William M. Bittle, who went on to own two other farms in the area. The proprietors of the Bittle stores in Myersville and Ellerton were related to the Bittles of Bittle Road. Note the classic drive-through barn in the photograph above. In the photograph below, the men and boys of the family, along with hired hands, are engaged in threshing, loosening chaff from the grain. (Both, courtesy of Debbie Wilson.)

NOV. 11, 1926

Hostess—Mrs. Smouse

Song—Sweet and Low
Roll Call
Response— Historical Places in Frederick County
Program in Charge of Legislation Committee, Miss Theo. H. Beachley, Chairman
Current Events—Hostess
Song—Softly Now the Light of Day

NOV. 25, 1926

Hostess—Mrs. Mary Wachtel

Song—Thanksgiving Song
Roll Call
Response—A Favorite Thanksgiving Dish, Christmas Suggestions— Miss Thompson
Current Events—Hostess
Song—An Autumn Lullaby

DEC. 9, 1926

Hostess—Mrs. Effie J. Dean

Song—Jingle Bells
Roll Call
Response—Gifts you Would Like to Receive
Program in Charge Fine Arts Committee—Mrs. Walter Falkenstein, Chairman
Current Events—Hostess
Song—Christmas Carol

DEC. 23, 1926

Hostess—Miss Mary Muck

Song—Hark, the Herald Angels Sing
Roll Call
Response—How do You expect to Spend Christmas Day
Miss Thompson, Food requirements for all ages
Current Events—Hostess
Song—Holy Night

JAN. 13, 1926

Hostess—Mrs. John Eldridge

Song—Love's Old Sweet Song
Roll Call
Response—Favorite Winter Sport
Program in Charge of Education Committee—Miss Mary Muck, Chairman
Current Events—Hostess
Song—Juanita

JAN. 27, 1927

Hostess—Mrs. Harlen Wachtel

Song—Ben Bolt
Roll Call
Response—Your Hobby
Miss Thompson—Curtains and Draperies
Current Events—Hostess
Song—The Spanish Cavalier

FEB. 10, 1927

Hostess—Miss Rhoda Eldridge

Song—Columbia the Gem of the Ocean
Roll Call
Response—Reminiscences of Abraham Lincoln's Boyhood Days
Program in Charge Public Welfare Committee—Mrs. Jack Mause, Chairman
Current Events—Hostess
Song—The Battle Cry of Freedom

FEB. 24, 1927

Hostess—Mrs. Clyde Wachtel

Song—America
Roll Call
Response—Something you've read about Washington
Miss Thompson— (Demonstration) New Soups
Current Events—Hostess
Song—My Bonnie

MARCH 10, 1927

Hostess—Mrs. John Langdon

Song—The Wearing of the Green
Roll Call

The Woman's Club, a branch of the Grange, was a large and popular organization in Middletown Valley towns. The motto of the Myersville Woman's Club was "Labor Conquers Everything." The program above outlines the agenda for meetings during the winter of 1926–1927. Area women's clubs later merged with local homemakers clubs. (Courtesy of Middletown Valley Historical Society.)

Myersville fielded town baseball teams as early as the late 1800s and held heated matches with squads from each of the neighboring communities. In this early photograph, two of the town's players stand in their woolen uniforms on Main Street. The Lawson Bittle store is behind them on the left, and the Farmers Mutual Exchange is on the right. (Courtesy of Debbie Wilson.)

Six

Wolfsville

In the 1960s, as the country was experiencing a turbulent social revolution, well-known Wolfsviller Cecil Martin asked an elderly local farmer for his views on the secret of happiness. "One thing you've gotta say for a place like this: it's doggone hard for a man to starve here," said the old fellow. "Happiness—well, I guess it's a matter of livin' as near right as you can and not wantin' too much you know you can't get."

Early settlers, attracted by the fertile land and rolling hills, moved into the area around what is now Wolfsville in the mid-1700s. The town itself got its impetus from John Hoover, a distant ancestor of Pres. Herbert Hoover, who acquired a huge tract of land and established the town's first church in a newly erected barn in 1819.

Wolfsville has always been a quiet place. But like so many of the communities in the Middletown Valley, the silence was shattered for a time during the Civil War. Once the excitement passed, farmers returned to their fields, children attended one-room schools—when they weren't helping out at the home place—people resumed enterprises such as shoemaking, blacksmithing, and tanning, and folks returned to their daily lives of hard work, churchgoing, and traditional rural get-togethers.

In ensuing years, everyday life was punctuated by developments such as the establishment of a hotel in the nearby hills, the inauguration of an annual town picnic, publication of a short-lived newspaper, and the formation of town bands and baseball teams. It was not until the 1930s that the main roads were paved, farms were electrified, and advanced mechanization became widespread. Around that time, the small one-room schools were shuttered, and students were sent to the newly constructed elementary school in Wolfsville. The town's high school was closed, and the children were taken by buses and trolleys to Middletown, some 12 miles away.

But as much as life was changing, it somehow, in essence, remained the same. Despite the influx of "outsiders," increased motorized transport, and new means of communication—telephone, radio, and television—Wolfsville and its surrounding areas have remained stubbornly serene.

The traditional German bank barn above was built in 1819 by John and Susannah Hoover, the son and daughter-in-law of one of the founders of the Wolfsville United Brethren congregation. Until they built a stone dwelling across the road the following year, the family lived in the log building below. The log home was constructed in the 1770s and stood until it was demolished in the mid-1980s. The barn served as a meetinghouse for big meetings of United Brethren residents until a church was built in 1847. The 100th anniversary of the Salem Church was celebrated in the Hoover barn, and special church services are still conducted there. (Both, courtesy of anonymous.)

In addition to serving as a residence, John and Susannah Hoover's stone home (above) was used for regular services of Wolfsville's United Brethren congregation until the Salem Church was built in 1847. In the late 1800s, it became a summer resort and boardinghouse called the Hoover House. It is the oldest standing residential structure in Wolfsville. (Courtesy of anonymous.)

STILL AT THE

OLD AND RELIABLE STAND,

NO. 2 HOOVER STREET,

Wolfsville, Md.

Having just returned from the city with a general assortment of very cheap goods, we are prepared to sell at prices that

Will Astonish You

When compared with the price of a year ago. It is surely dropping the old, worn-out song and singing a new one on a very low key, and we propose to sell goods on the

SAME KEY NOTE

To all persons—rich or poor—as all money is of the same value. If you wish to deal on that plan, call at the

HOOVER HOUSE,

Where business is done honorably and in a satisfactory manner.

DRY GOODS.

Best Calicoes, from 5c to 6c; Dress Goods, such as Poplins and Delains, from 8 to 16c; Muslins as low as 4c per yard; Cottonades as low as 10c per yard; best Whittenton, 24c per yard, C. K.; Gentlemen's Socks, Ladies Stockings, Handkerchiefs and Japanese Fans—all for 5c each; Ladies' and Gentlemen's Gloves for 12c to 15c per pair; Gent's Cravats, from 15c to 25c; Sun Umbrellas, from 40c to 50c.

GROCERIES.

O. K. Roasted Coffee, 17c per lb.; Rio Coffee, 2 pounds for 25c; N. C. Rice, 10c. per pound; Golden Syrup, 50c per gal.; Calvert, 44c per gal.; New Orleans, 60c per gal.; Chewing Tobacco for 50c a lb.; Fancy Soaps, from 1c to 7c per cake.

DRUGS OR MEDICINES at unusually low rates.

Grateful for past custom, I would be thankful for future patronage.

I remain, yours, truly,

JOHN W. HOOVER.

Globe Pr., Hagerstown, Md.

John W. Hoover operated a general store in the late 1800s and issued this enthusiastic announcement to let prospective customers know that he had "just returned from the city with a general assortment of very cheap goods, we are prepared to sell at prices that Will Astonish You." (Author's collection.)

The building above, in the center of Wolfsville, was constructed about 1870 and was used by John Donohoo as a store selling shoes, fabrics, lamps, tobacco, and general goods until 1888. The second floor served as a meeting hall and, for a time, the Wolfsville high school. The building also housed a medical practice. In 1927, Asa Stottlemyer moved his automobile repair business (below) to the property, making alterations to the structure over the years. He opened a general store in the building in 1934 and ran it until his death in 1971. (Both, courtesy of George Harne.)

The former Milton Harne store at the square in Wolfsville dates back to the 1800s and was operated by a succession of local proprietors. Milton Harne and his wife, Catherine, purchased the store for $3,000 in 1943 and operated it for 45 years. Their son George and his wife, Judith, continued to run it until 2009. Catherine eventually decided to forgo retirement and worked in the store until 2005. (Courtesy of George Harne.)

In 1934, in the midst of the Great Depression, Lee Delauter bought a log home near Middlepoint and began selling animal feed from a storefront on the ground floor. He added groceries, a gas station, and other goods as he constructed additions to the original structure. The business has continued to expand under the leadership of his sons. In this photograph, his son Dale stands in front of the Delauter store. (Courtesy of Dale Delauter.)

Even small villages in the Middletown Valley had a square, which served as a center for commercial activity. At the crossing between two roads, Wolfsville's square featured stores and some residences. In this 1943 photograph, Asa Stottlemyer's service station and store and the Milton Harne general store were the prime businesses in downtown Wolfsville. (Courtesy of the Draper family.)

As noted earlier, loafing was a time-honored tradition throughout the Middletown Valley. In this photograph from the early 1940s, regulars are gathered on the porch of Asa Stottlemyer's general store in Wolfsville to trade news, stories, and opinions. (Courtesy of the Draper family.)

The original Salem United Brethren in Christ Church (above) was built in 1847 and remains part of the complex today. In 1893, the church was rebuilt to repair and replace parts of the structure. An education building was added in 1967 where the old Wolfsville School had once stood. Through denominational mergers, the congregation became Evangelical Brethren in Christ in 1946 and United Methodist in 1968. (Courtesy of Patricia Wolfe.)

When St. Mark's Lutheran Church (right) was built in 1847, it was a one-room stone structure. As was traditional, two doors led into the church, one for women and one for men. The congregation became part of the St. John's charge when it united with the Church Hill congregation in 1850. (Courtesy of anonymous.)

The gentleman stepping into the carriage in this early 1900s photograph is likely Dr. Alvey J. Smith, who was a familiar figure around the area, traveling by horse and buggy to make house calls with his small medical satchel. The man standing behind the carriage is believed to be Asbury Hoover, who was the local distributor for Black Diamond Liniment, a widely used anesthetic for animal wounds and sores. (Courtesy of George Harne.)

Rural children learned all aspects of farming beginning at an early age. In this Wolfsville photograph from the 1940s, a young boy is shown the proper technique for picking a chicken to prepare it for cooking. (Courtesy of the Draper family.)

Members of the Draper family stretch and skin a possum on their farm near Wolfsville in 1942. A sharp knife and years of tradition-borne expertise were required to do the job right. (Courtesy of the Draper family.)

Butchering time at the home place was an occasion for family and friends to gather to slaughter some of the livestock and prepare meat for the coming months. It was also a social occasion, capped by hearty meals and lots of animated conversation. (Courtesy of the Draper family.)

"Belsnickling" was a popular tradition in the Wolfsville area until the mid-20th century. During the week between Christmas and New Year's Day, adults and children disguised in face masks would knock on doors around the valley in an attempt to surprise and perhaps frighten neighbors. After guessing each belsnickler's identity, treats and cider were served. This 1940 photograph shows members of the Kuhn family dressed up for belsnickling. (Courtesy of the Draper family.)

The Wolfsville School (above) stood near the cemetery of the St. James Reformed Church close to what is now Black Rock Road. The two-room school was heated by potbellied stoves, which burned wood and eventually coal. In 1915, a new brick school was built near the Salem United Methodist Church (below). In an article about the old Wolfsville School, former student Kenneth Frushour noted that teachers during this era were permitted to employ the hickory stick. He recalled, "Mr. Leatherman's 'Board of Education' . . . was about thirty inches long, having a tapered handle and having several holes drilled in the opposite end of the handle . . . to make it more effective as a deterrent of misbehaving." Frushour eventually became principal of Wolfsville Elementary School. (Both, courtesy of the Draper family.)

The Forrest School (above), north of Wolfsville in Garfield, was built in 1882. It contained two rooms, one for grades one through three and the other for grades four through seven. Girls and boys sat on separate sides of each room, and poor behavior was punished by exile to the area occupied by the opposite gender. Two potbellied stoves heated the rooms, and water was hauled in by the older boys from a nearby spring. The photograph below shows the Forrest School's two teachers from 1914 to 1917, Rooklyn Pryor and William Harne. Harne taught at the school for 25 years. Forrest School closed in 1939, and students were transferred to the Wolfsville School. (Both, courtesy of George Harne.)

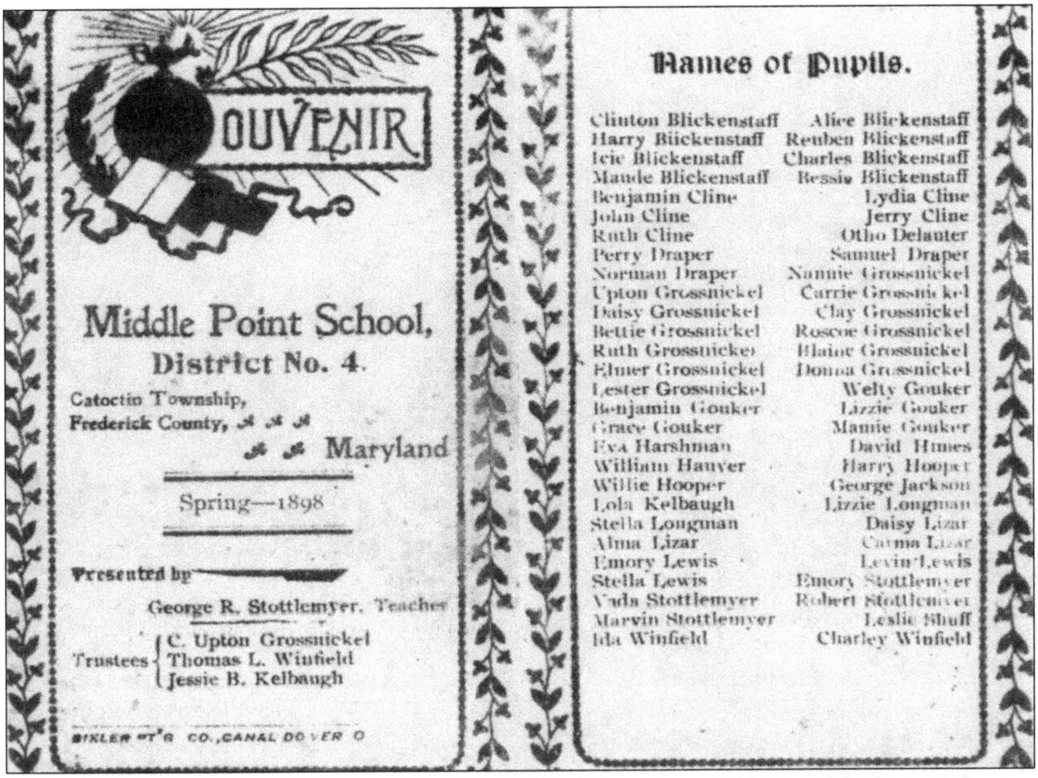

SOUVENIR

Middle Point School,
District No. 4.
Catoctin Township,
Frederick County,
Maryland

Spring—1898

Presented by
George R. Stottlemyer, Teacher

Trustees: C. Upton Grossnickel, Thomas L. Winfield, Jessie B. Kelbaugh

Bixler Pt'g Co., Canal Dover O

Names of Pupils.

Clinton Blickenstaff	Alice Blickenstaff
Harry Biickenstaff	Reuben Blickenstaff
Icie Blickenstaff	Charles Blickenstaff
Maude Blickenstaff	Bessie Blickenstaff
Benjamin Cline	Lydia Cline
John Cline	Jerry Cline
Ruth Cline	Otho Delauter
Perry Draper	Samuel Draper
Norman Draper	Nannie Grossnickel
Upton Grossnickel	Carrie Grossnickel
Daisy Grossnickel	Clay Grossnickel
Bettie Grossnickel	Roscoe Grossnickel
Ruth Grossnickel	Blaine Grossnickel
Elmer Grossnickel	Donna Grossnickel
Lester Grossnickel	Welty Gouker
Benjamin Gouker	Lizzie Gouker
Grace Gouker	Mamie Gouker
Eva Harshman	David Himes
William Hauver	Harry Hooper
Willie Hooper	George Jackson
Lola Kelbaugh	Lizzie Longman
Stella Longman	Daisy Lizar
Alma Lizar	Carma Lizar
Emory Lewis	Levin Lewis
Stella Lewis	Emory Stottlemyer
Vada Stottlemyer	Robert Stottlemyer
Marvin Stottlemyer	Leslie Shuff
Ida Winfield	Charley Winfield

The original Middlepoint School, located between Ellerton and Wolfsville, operated from at least the mid-1800s. The program above celebrates the spring 1898 term and lists the names of 56 students. The second Middlepoint School was constructed at the same location in 1906 and closed around 1924. The building was moved and became a residence on the road between Middletown and Jefferson. (Courtesy of the Draper family.)

Morgan's Mill operated for 85 years on Brandenburg Hollow Road. James Wesley Morgan established the business in 1881 and made kitchen cupboards, beds, bureaus, tables, and chests. The mill was operated by family members until it closed in 1966. The Wolfsville Ruritan Club later purchased the property and established a community park. (Courtesy of the Draper family.)

Wolfsville has a rich musical heritage. A 1972 history of the area notes that no fewer than six bands and two orchestras operated between the 1880s and the 1950s. In the faded photograph from the early 1900s above, members of the Stottlemyer Orchestra are gathered on the porch of Fred Stottlemyer in Wolfsville for a practice session. Bands played at area festivals, performed concerts, and marched in local parades. In the undated photograph at left, the Wolfsville Band marches in a parade down Pleasant Walk Road. (Above, courtesy of Harold Stotelmyer; left, courtesy of anonymous.)

One of the most treasured items a Middletown Valley resident can possess is a genuine Stottlemyer rocking chair, like the one at right. Christopher Columbus Stottlemyer established a small factory (above) near Wolfsville in the early 1900s and created what many describe as the most comfortable, durable rockers ever made. The factory also made straight-back chairs, stools, benches, and other items. Stottlemyer was aided in the construction process by his five sons. His wife and two daughters wove the splint backs and bottoms of the chairs. Stottlemyer learned the chair-making craft from his father, Frederick, who, it is believed, made the rocker at right between 1850 and 1885. C.C. Stottlemyer stopped making furniture when he was stricken with paralysis in 1931, but members of his family have continued the woodworking tradition. (Both, courtesy of Dorothy Buhrman.)

Shortly after the Civil War, Jacob Wolf decided to take advantage of the area's climate and scenery and built a hotel in the mountains outside of Wolfsville, which he called Black Rock Hotel. Unfortunately, the hotel burned in 1880. In 1907, his son Jacob Drill Wolf, freshly returned from unsuccessful commercial ventures in New York, rebuilt the hotel on the same site (above). The new building was constructed of native stone and had a kitchen and dining room on the first floor and a total of 17 rooms on the second and third floors. The remote location and poor roads led to the enterprise's demise, and the building fell into disrepair. However, hikers and picnickers enjoyed climbing around in its remains (below). Today, the ruins are a stopping point for hikers on the Appalachian Trail. (Above, courtesy of Western Maryland Room; below, courtesy of the Draper family.)

The Middlepoint covered bridge, built in 1851 on Spruce Run Road, survived until 1933, when it was replaced by a concrete span. A local resident later described the dismantling thusly: "The farmers got onto the roof and sawed the center beam and the sides fell into the creek. They pulled it out and took it home for firewood which the children called popcorn as it was so old and dry it snapped in the fireplace." (Courtesy of the Draper family.)

Like many shops in the valley, the general store in Garfield doubled as a home for its proprietor and his family. Walter Wolfe purchased the building from Upton Brandenburg in 1916 and operated it until his death in 1947. In winter, the extended family gathered in the basement for butchering. Local "belsnicklers" relied on the Wolfe Store to carry a variety of masks during the Christmas season. (Courtesy of the Draper family.)

www.ingramcontent.com/pod-product-compliance
Lightning Source LLC
LaVergne TN
LVHW081548100826
845153LV00004B/340